DREAMING IN
A NIGHTMARE

DREAMING IN A NIGHTMARE

Inequality and What We Can Do About It

Jeremiah Emmanuel

1 3 5 7 9 10 8 6 4 2

#Merky Books
20 Vauxhall Bridge Road
London SW1V 2SA

#Merky Books is part of the Penguin Random House group of companies
whose addresses can be found at global.penguinrandomhouse.com

Penguin
Random House
UK

First published by #Merky Books in 2020
This paperback edition published by #Merky Books in 2021

www.penguin.co.uk

A CIP catalogue record for this book is available from the British Library

ISBN 9781529118629

Printed and bound in Italy by Grafica veneta S.p.A.

The authorised representative in the EEA is Penguin Random House Ireland,
Morrison Chambers, 32 Nassau Street, Dublin D02 YH68

Penguin Random House is committed to a sustainable future
for our business, our readers and our planet. This book is made from
Forest Stewardship Council® certified paper.

For Gloria Green
Forever in our hearts

Author's Note

I have sometimes changed the names and details of individuals within the text to preserve anonymity, but everything you are about to read is true, or as close to the truth as I can tell it.

Contents

Contributor Biographies

Victor Acquah

Victor Acquah is a former investment banker turned entrepreneur. He consults for a number of businesses and individuals in the entertainment industry. He also secures key investment opportunities for his clients and assists in the delivery of events. In 2019 he helped put together an event at the O2 Arena with a 20,000 capacity. In his spare time Victor works as a commissioned officer the Army Cadet Force. He currently holds the rank of Captain.

Debbie Antwi

Debbie is a Partnerships Officer and Youth Worker who grew up in south London. She's passionate about helping young people, having worked in adventure playgrounds and youth clubs across Lambeth for almost ten years. Debbie believes that young people should have a say in the spaces they use. She currently works at Building Young Brixton with a focus on ensuring the services delivered are youth-led and regularly holds meetings with the Youth Steering Group. Outside of work, Debbie enjoys chilling with her fifteen nephews and nieces, reading and writing (having completed a master's in Children's Literature), and baking.

Esther Daniel

Esther Daniel is a church minister and children's pastor. Her life ambition has been to give back to others, and support the local community and beyond. She hopes to soon kick-start the organisation she founded fifteen years ago, 'Beauty4Ashes'.

Mariam Diaby

Mariam Diaby is a twenty-one-year-old social creative and activist from south-east London. She is currently in her third year of university studying Politics and IR and is committed to creating change within society. She is a part of the Damilola Trust Youth board, a charity which aims to improve and better communities, and is currently finishing a documentary focusing on young black boys and mental health. She is shortly launching MDTV, a channel that will produce insight into the reality of events that affect young people, whilst acknowledging individuals doing great things within our society.

Deborah Emmanuel

Deborah Emmanuel is a creative from Brixton, and the loving mother of Josiah. Deborah runs 'Hampers by Dee', a bespoke seasonal hamper business.

Krystal Frimpong

Krystal Frimpong is a British-born Ghanaian currently working in the construction and building management industry. Krystal has a BA honours in Marketing and Media and is a social activist, who has worked in the criminal justice system and mentored young children from various backgrounds. She is passionate about supporting young people and helping them to fulfil their limitless potential. In her spare time, Krystal supports event management, contributes to documentaries and podcasts, and bakes. Krystal is focused on a diverse and inclusive community that fosters progress.

Seven Jacobs

Seven is a social entrepreneur and innovator. Having worked with brands like Nando's, Superdry, Nike, and Instagram, and being an advocate within charities and for wellbeing, mental health and meaningful self discovery, he runs unique workshops and gives talks through his own brands, enterprises, and projects. Growing up feeling isolated by the systems meant to support you, he is a strong proponent for building programmes and relationships to give young people meaningful voice and opportunities.

Karl Lokko

Karl Lokko is a former gang leader turned activist, poet, public speaker, adventurer and personal advisor. Further to this he has managed to harness his life experiences which has propelled and uniquely situated him as an activist and influencer within the UK. Karl is a gifted orator with a rare ability to connect with people on a human level, bridging worlds and uniting communities.

Damani Mensah

Damani Mensah is a twenty-one-year-old entrepreneur from south London. He is an A&R scout at Just Entertainment and music manager. He is also the tour manager for up-and-coming artist Frosty. His aim is to one day start his own music management consultancy company.

Precious Oyelade

Precious Oyelade is a writer and marketer who has worked and volunteered in education, media and tech. She graduated with a degree in Politics, Psychology and Sociology from the University of Cambridge, and received a starred first for her dissertation on the impact of Nollywood – Nigerian film – on the Nigerian UK diaspora. She was later awarded the University of London Award upon completing her MA in African Studies at SOAS. She is currently working in communications, specialising in African tech, sits on the youth advisory board for CVQO – a vocational education charity, and consults for an African diaspora entertainment channel in the UK.

Daryl Parker

Daryl Parker is a qualified personal trainer, nutrition coach and entrepreneur from Croydon. He studied Sports Science at Coventry University, and currently runs his own online personal training company, www. darylparker.co.uk

Introduction

'All my life I've had dreams in a nightmare, because where I'm from there's no scenery and no sun. I've just tried to work hard for Mum. I'm just a young entrepreneur who's trying to change the world!'

23 October 2017

Welcome to *Dreaming in a Nightmare*. My name is Jeremiah Emmanuel. I'm twenty years old and I was born and raised in south London. All my life, I've felt like I've inhabited two different worlds. In one, I am listened to and respected. Doors are opened for me. I can do anything I want to. In another, I am ignored and I am targeted. In this world, prison is expected and violence is accepted. I have no opportunities and am punished for thinking I might succeed. This is a book about my life, but it's about your life too. It's about those two worlds – the dream and the nightmare – how you can move between them, and what happens when you do.

You are probably wondering what I mean. Well, let me give you a few examples . . .

Scene one. I'm fifteen years old, waiting outside 10 Downing Street to receive an award for my community work. I'm a little nervous, but excited. I'm wearing a suit that's a bit too big for me. The award was called Points of Light – an award that's given out by the prime minister (and the president in the USA) to a volunteer who is making a positive difference in their community. I eventually got inside, met David Cameron, stood around chatting to various inspiring people, and had a few photographs taken. It was a good day.

Later that week, I was walking in my area on my own, and I was stopped by two police officers, one male and one female. They took me in the back of their van and made me take some of my clothes off in order to search me.

I couldn't see why I had been singled out, but it was not a new experience. If I'm ever out with my friends and we see a police van pass, we play a game where we start counting to see how many seconds it will take before we're stopped. I think the last time was ten seconds. I understand that police officers have a job to do. Maybe that's why sometimes I just let it happen. It's normal. It's normal when you talk to your friends about it afterwards. It's normal when you see it happening to someone else. It's normal until you start talking about it with people who don't experience it. It's normal until you realise it's not normal. Then it becomes something else. It becomes strange and shocking and upsetting. It's degrading. It's painful. It makes you feel worthless.

I remember thinking, as all of this was happening, how mad it was. A few days ago I had been with the prime minister in 10 Downing Street and now I'm being treated like I'm nothing, pulled off the street and humiliated in the back of a police van for no apparent reason. I have tried to make a positive change in my community and this is the way I am treated. This is the way I am always treated. This is the reality.

Scene two. Fast forward a year or two, and I was going through a bit of a difficult time. I was thinking a lot about my life, what I had done, and what I wanted to do next. How to properly escape the nightmare, really. Fate intervened, or so it seemed. For a long time I'd been applying for various grants and bursaries to continue my education and, a few weeks later, I found out that I was being awarded a full scholarship to go to university from an amazing organisation called the Amos Bursary (look them up!). They were offering to pay all my tuition fees — something like £27,000 in total. It was an extraordinary opportunity. A dream. But at the same time, I wasn't sure if I was really ready.

I decided to go and see a friend who works for a charity in central London to ask for some advice, but the day before I was supposed to meet her, I got a call. One of my best friends, Kyle, had been stabbed and was in hospital. He had been waiting in the queue outside a show and a fight had broken out. He was there with a lot of his friends and it turned out that some other boys from a different area had spotted them. There was no animosity towards Kyle but because he was with this particular group, he was a target. As the fight broke out, people started screaming and running away. (This is what happens if you hear screaming in the ends, you don't run towards it, you run away. This was a lesson I had to learn the hard way.) So everyone ran and it just so happens that Kyle ended up on his own. He was rushed. This group of boys got him down and stabbed him seven times, mostly in his arms and legs.

Kyle was lucky. He suffered damage to some of the tendons in his legs, which means that he is still recovering to this day, but it could have been so much worse. I rushed to the hospital and sat with him, talking for a while. I think he was in that early stage of shock where he couldn't quite make sense of what had happened. He was talking normally, which was a little odd in itself. The ward was filled with patients who were seriously ill, or dying. You could hear other visitors whispering and crying. Kyle was adamant that he wouldn't let the experience change him. He was determined to turn it into a positive, somehow. I was just happy he was still alive.

Kyle happened to be in a hospital just around the corner from where my friend worked at the charity. After I saw him I walked over to visit her. We sat in her office overlooking the Thames, talking about the scholarship offer and what I should do next. She said to me, 'Look Jeremiah, if you decide not to take it, there's always a job for you here.' It clicked. I thought university was something I *should* do, rather than something I really wanted to do. If I worked at the charity, I believed I could make a difference. So I said yes.

Scene three. I am on the terrace of a restaurant in Corsica, overlooking the sea. It's early evening and the sun is beginning to set. I am sitting at a table with a group of thirty people, including various CEOs, entrepreneurs, investors, policy-makers and philanthropists. We had spent the past two days cycling across the island together at an annual fundraising event, designed to bring leading figures from different arenas together in the name of charity.

My mum often likes to berate me by listing the accomplishments of my friends or the children of her friends. Anyone with West African parents, most likely anyone with a pushy mum, will know what I'm talking about.

'Did you hear that Cynthia's daughter has just graduated? When are you going to go to university?' 'Anthony
has got a job in the city. He's earning a lot. When will you
get a proper job?' 'Mary's son is taking her on holiday
next week. It must be so nice to have a son who would do
that for his mother . . .'. And so on and so on. But in addition, my mum has always paraded the accomplishments
of Richard Branson as a kind of incentive. It is weird.
Maybe she sees some of the same things in both of us, I
don't know, but I heard his name *a lot* growing up.

Anyway, also at this dinner in Corsica was none other
than Richard Branson. After the meal we somehow got
chatting on the balcony. It was too good an opportunity to miss. 'Richard,' I asked. 'Would you mind saying
hello to my mum, if I quickly FaceTimed her?' Luckily
he agreed. I called my mum and handed the phone
over, much to her shock. It wasn't a lot really, I was just
standing next to the guy, but it was a moment I will
never forget; leaning on the railing of that balcony in
Corsica overlooking the sea, watching Richard Branson
and my mum talk and laugh on the telephone. The
dream. Do you know what I mean?

Now I need to backtrack a little. I have a cousin named
Kayla (we're not actually related, but we're so close that
we call each other cousins, if that makes any sense). We
speak all the time but, for some reason, it's never
on the telephone. WhatsApp, Instagram, Twitter, in

person — but never on the telephone. Kayla is still friendly with a lot of people from school and a lot of people from the ends, and has become a kind of unofficial source of news and updates. Not a gossip as such, but someone who likes to keep tabs on everyone. So, Kayla never calls me. She will only call me if something bad has happened.

Two days before the trip to Corsica, I got a call from Kayla. I was at home, I remember. She said, 'Have you heard? Aaron is dead.'

Aaron was a friend of mine from school. He was funny, always making jokes, always the class clown. He was clever, but his behaviour got worse as we grew up and in year eleven, before our GCSEs, he got kicked out and sent to a pupil referral unit (or PRU). We'll come back to this later on in the education chapter, but it's enough to know for now that PRUs are not a good thing. Nearly everyone I knew who went to a PRU is in prison or dead.

So, I hadn't seen Aaron much, but we'd kept in touch until very recently. He'd just come out of prison for some foolishness — he'd got in an argument with a shopkeeper and ended up slapping him. Six months for GBH. I wrote to him once or twice and he was in prison with another good friend of mine, so we stayed connected. Don't get me wrong, I knew that he was getting caught up in various bad things, but he was a good person. I am not excusing his behaviour, but I can understand why he ended up where he did and I hope by the time you finish this book, you will too.

Anyway, not long after his release, Aaron had been out with the wrong friend in the wrong area. This is never a good idea and, at that time, was a particularly bad one. There had been a number of altercations in the neighbourhood and everyone was on the lookout for trouble. Aaron and his friend were spotted and rushed by a group of boys with knives. They ran, but Aaron was caught. In those kinds of situations, it's really kill or be killed. Aaron was killed.

His friend came back to see what had happened and found Aaron lying on the side of the road on his own. Aaron had been stabbed a lot — in his back, his chest, his stomach. His friend somehow managed to get him into a taxi and that's where he died. About two minutes away from a hospital. Stuck in traffic on a south London road.

The next morning, I got the call from Kayla. This is two days before I was supposed to fly out to Corsica. I thought about not going, but in the end, it felt like there was nothing I could achieve by staying in London. So I went. Aaron's funeral was held the morning after the dinner on the terrace, where my mum had spoken to Richard Branson. I locked myself in my room with my phone and kept up with what was happening with my friends who were there. I think there was something like 200 people at the church. It was a strange and very sad situation. How do you come to terms with death when you're eighteen? I just thought about all the things I had done with Aaron, and all the things we would never do together. I was never going to see him again. He would never make it to twenty. He would never move out, get married or have kids. He would never have the opportunity to turn his life around. After the funeral I left my hotel room and joined the rest of the group. I didn't say a word about what had happened. How could I?

*

Picture a group of boys sitting dangerously close to the edge of a small building. They are not safe. There is a pair of legs sticking out at an odd angle. One of the boys is bracing himself at the edge, looking down in fear. Another boy is clinging on, about to fall. No one is trying to help him. You worry about these boys. Maybe you think they are up to no good.

When I was young, we used to look up at our elders and think they were mad. Guys who were getting arrested, getting kicked out of school, carrying weapons, selling drugs. It was crazy. It was crazy, but it was expected.

This image represents the struggle that a lot of people in my generation have to face. We are alone on the edge of a precipice. There's no safety net.

There is also clouds and blue sky. It's the beginning of a dream. A group of boys are climbing up on to a rooftop to enjoy the sun. You can almost hear the laughter. It's the summer. They are carefree. This is escape. The horizon stretches away without end. Anything is possible. Maybe you want to be with them. Back when I was that age, we had no worries. We were just kids enjoying our lives. Even though we didn't come from the best of environments, we still had a good time.

The dream is a way out. It's like an exit plan. It's a vision of a better life. I feel from when we were young we recognised that we were stuck in a cycle. We got to a certain age and we thought, Is this it? Life got real. So we had to dream. It was the only way we could get out of this life. The dream is your way out.

I always used to dream. I dreamed about moving out of the area, finding somewhere better to live. I dreamed about doing something with my life. But those dreams didn't necessarily correlate with my reality. These were dreams I shouldn't have been having. We were told to be ordinary, when we wanted to be extraordinary. I had to dream because no one else was dreaming for me.

The nightmare is that closed-off space. It's a lack of opportunity. It's that feeling of 'Is this it?' It's talking to people about the reality of life and seeing a look of shock or disgust on their faces. The nightmare is a world without opportunity or possibilities. It's being stuck. The nightmare is not a physical place. It's a state of mind. You are living in a nightmare if you are letting your background, your environment or people's perceptions limit your potential.

This is all getting a bit woolly, I realise. Let me be specific. Although people of any age can be living in a nightmare, this is an issue that primarily affects a younger generation. A recent report by the *Financial Times* found that millenials are the first generation in over a century to be, on average, less wealthy than their parents at a similar age. You can call me a snowflake all you want, but it's an undisputed fact that young people today have fewer opportunities and more pressure than ever before. According to the Equality and Human Rights Commission's five-year report, the percentage of young people aged sixteen to twenty-four living in poverty has increased. The average hourly earnings of young people has declined, in real terms. In England, young people are more likely than any other age group to live in unsatisfactory housing. Young people are less likely to be employed and more likely to be the victims of violent crime. In another report from the Office of National Statistics, it showed that the proportion of young people reporting symptoms of anxiety or depression increased from 18 per cent in 2009/2010 to 21 per cent in 2013/2014. The number of young people who said that they had someone to rely a lot on decreased from 80 per cent in 2010/2011 to 76 per cent in 2013/2014. That's almost one in four young people who do not feel they have someone they can rely on.

Of course, the struggles you face in life, and the chances you have, aren't just affected by age. I am a young black boy from south London. As much as I want this book to be of help to all young people who are struggling, it is written from that perspective, because that is what I know. Being a young black person in Britain means that you have additional obstacles to face. As the saying goes, you have to work twice as hard to get half as far. That is something I have experienced first-hand.

But a lot of the issues I have faced are common to a lot of young people across the country. Don't get me wrong, being a young black person in Britain is hard. But no matter your race, your gender or your sexual orientation, if you are under the age of twenty-four and come from a particular socio-economic background, you are likely to struggle.

For a large part of my life I was living in a nightmare. But I never stopped dreaming. And today, God willing, I am living in a dream. I want to use my life as a guide. Not because I know everything, because I really don't. But I have always felt like I've seen and done some things that I hope can help others.

I proved to myself that I don't have to be a product of my background or my environment. This is not a book about how bad life is. This is a book about hope. This is a guide to recognising the nightmare – and a blueprint for dreaming your way out of it.

1

Identity

My mother's story

I have a good friend called Kenny, a social entrepreneur who has worked on a number of charitable projects with a man named Lord Hastings. Lord Hastings was, Kenny told me, a life peer, the Head of Global Citizenship at KPMG, and a former head of public affairs at the BBC. A big deal. Fast-forward a few months; I was speaking at an event in London. As I came offstage, a black man, maybe around sixty years old, came over to say hello and to ask me about my speech. We had a chat, and at the end he handed me his business card. It said, 'Dr Michael Hastings, Baron Hastings of Scarisbrick, CBE'. I couldn't believe it. I said, 'Lord Hastings!'

Whenever Kenny or others described him, I had always imagined him as white — a middle-aged upper-class white man. I had never thought he might be black. But he is. One of the 100 most influential black people in Britain, according to Wikipedia.

I wrote to him a few days later to thank him and he replied, saying, 'Jeremiah, I would love to know who you are.' I was a bit confused, as we had spoken a little bit about what I did, but I tried to explain: 'Dear Lord Hastings, my name is Jeremiah. We met backstage at the event the other day. I founded EMNL Consultancy, I'm a youth activist and entrepreneur . . .' and so on. He came back almost immediately: 'Jeremiah, I didn't ask what you *do*, I asked who you *are*.'

I remember staring at the email when it arrived. I couldn't get my head around it. It spun me. What did he mean? What else could I say? I'm Jeremiah! It took me a day or two before I could think about how to reply. Eventually I came up with, 'My name is Jeremiah. I was raised in a single-parent family. I come from a difficult environment. And I want to change the world for myself, and for everyone like me.' Or something like that, anyway . . .

It was a much better answer, and a more accurate one. Lord Hastings thought so too. He said: 'Thank you. I understand who you are now.'

Before that, I don't really think I knew who I was. I never really gave it any thought. I'm not sure many people my age do. Who you are and what you do are two very different things. This is a question of identity; it's an important question. We don't know who we are. And that can have significant impacts in the short and long term.

*

The first question I would like to ask is: who are you? The second question to ask is: who do people think you are? The third question is: which is true?

These answers will shape every aspect of your life.

As I said to Lord Hastings, I was brought up in a single-parent household. We didn't have much. I am also a young, curious, ambitious person. I believe in my community. I believe in my friends. I would also describe myself as British. Ignore for now the fact that I only became a British citizen many years after I was born here. I'm a citizen. I am British. But if someone asked me where I'm from, I don't think I would say Britain, and definitely not England. Not first of all, anyway. Does that make sense? It's a fact that is also true for a lot of my friends. They may be second or third-generation Jamaicans or Ghanaians or Bahamians, but they'll name those countries before Britain or England, if they're ever asked where they're from.

My family are from Nigeria, so I'd say that I was Nigerian before I'm anything else, and there are a few obvious and less obvious reasons for that. Just to be clear, I have never actually visited Nigeria. The first time I stepped foot on the continent of Africa was in 2017. But growing up in the diaspora and being around Nigerian culture, I nevertheless feel like a part of the country. That I can justifiably and proudly call myself Nigerian. It's not necessarily a loyalty to Nigeria, it's more an indisputable fact that it's a part of who I am. It's where my parents come from, so in a way I come from there too. Saying that, I've got some friends whose parents were born in England, but they still refuse to identify as English.

I think this is also true for many people of my age. A recent YouGov survey found that 72 per cent of people aged 65 and over identify as English, and are proud of that identity. For 18–24 year-olds, that number drops to 45 per cent. Close to 10 per cent of all young people interviewed said that they are 'actively embarrassed' about their Englishness.

Even if I called myself British or English, would the people around me? Would society at large? Afua Hirsch wrote an extraordinary book, *Brit(ish)*, about this question (I recommend you read it as soon as you can). As she said in an article on its subject:

Britain is my home, my nationality, my frame of reference. I've spoken its language all my life — correct, middle-class, Thames Estuary English. I have studied at Oxford, been called to the Bar. I've both aspired to be part of its institutions, and been institutionalised by its aspirations. And yet this country of mine had never allowed me to feel that it is where I belong. If I were to single out the most persistent reminder of that sense of not belonging, it would be The Question: 'Where are you from?' Although I have lived in five different countries as an adult, nowhere have I been asked The Question more than right here, where I am from, in Britain.

'Where are you from?' is a question I have been asked many times. This is 'who other people *think* you are'. And quite often, it's an outsider. I have always struggled with imposter syndrome: the feeling that you don't belong, that you're not good enough, that somehow you've tricked everyone into believing that you are better than you actually are. It's something that I think is part and parcel of being a person of colour living in Britain. It also connects to the idea of dreaming in a nightmare. I've always felt like I'm living two different lives. I'm the Jeremiah who can go to 10 Downing Street to receive an award from the prime minister, and simultaneously the Jeremiah who pulls his jogging bottoms down in the back of a police van. I'm Jeremiah who was born in Britain, but who isn't recognised as British. I've felt out of place for most of my life.

This chapter is about those two questions. Who I am versus who people think I am. But to answer both questions properly, I really need to start with what made me.

*

I have always been interested in music. I'm not sure how I got into it exactly, but I can remember music being played at home from my earliest years. Gospel definitely ruled the household, followed by Afrobeat and even grime. I remember being very young watching Channel U, trying to mimic each rapper as they delivered their verses. I was lucky enough to be encouraged to do more than just listen, however. By the age of ten, I had learned how to play four instruments (two quite badly), and at one point even managed to become the lead singer in two youth choirs.

Eventually, just like a lot of young people, my interest in practising and performing started to decline by the time I hit my teenage years. My voice also dropped an octave or two, so I could no longer hold those high notes in the Christmas carols. I continued to listen to music and, if anything, listened to it more and more as I got older. I'm very pleased and grateful that music is still an important part of my life. I set up and run a multi-purpose entertainment company called Just Entertainment, or JE, along with my good friend Kelvin Okogwu. I've always been up to date with my music, always on the lookout for new talent, but I like to think that I'm still a listener, first and foremost.

I love a wide variety of music from a number of different genres, but last year, the genre I loved the most was undoubtedly Afrobeats. Like a lot of people, I became obsessed. Back in 2012, Dan Hancox, writing in the *Guardian*, accurately predicted the rise of Afrobeats:

> Most people are familiar with the Afrobeat styles of Fela Kuti – Afrobeats is something different; with the addition of the letter 's' comes a whole new chapter in global pop music . . . a 21st century melting pot of western rap influences, and contemporary Ghanaian and Nigerian pop music.

The genre has grown rapidly from its humble beginnings in London, and is now shaping the sound of pop music on both sides of the Atlantic and beyond. Some of the most notable musicians in the genre today include Wiz Kid, Davido, Naira Marley, Fuse ODG, Sarkodie and my personal favourite, Burna Boy, Damini Ogulu. Burna, one of the few musicians I listen to on almost a daily basis, released his fourth studio album, *African*

Giant, on 26 July 2019. (You might think I'm taking a bit of a detour here, but bear with me. We'll get to the question of identity in a moment.) *African Giant* is a masterpiece, and a collection of songs that resonate with me for a several reasons. It's an album that lives up to its title; a swaggering, soulful, wide-ranging collection that points to a future for Afrobeats, but does not forget its past. You'll hear echoes of Caribbean dancehall, some grime braggadocio, a bit of sweet R&B ('Pull Up' and 'Secret', in particular) and, of course, the funk and jazz rhythms of classic Afrobeat. More than anything, as soon as I heard it, the album became a powerful reminder to me that I needed to learn about my roots.

I am a young black man, born in Britain. My family come from Nigeria. But as I said before, I have never visited the country. Instead, until very recently, I relied on my relatives, the diaspora and the very visible elements of Nigerian culture present in the UK to help me understand and connect to my heritage: the music, the dress, the food, the language. My family come from the Yoruba tribe, for example. I can still understand Yoruba when I hear it, but I'm unable to speak it. When I think about it now, Nigeria has always been an important part of who I am, but not something I ever really bothered to think about in a deeper way.

The first time I listened to Burna's album, there was one tune in particular that stood out. 'Another Story' begins

with a voice: 'To understand Nigeria, you need to appreciate where it came from . . . ' The song then cuts to an
extract from a documentary. It sounds like something
from the 1950s; a clipped, posh, British accent reeling
off a list of facts: 'In 1900, Britain officially assumed
responsibility for the administration of the whole of what
we now know as Nigeria, from the Niger company . . . '
What follows is a shocking and illuminating account of
Nigeria's recent past, a history lesson I had never received
in school, yet one that had so much to teach me about
who I am and where I come from. In order to understand my story, I not only needed to understand my
mother's story. I needed to understand the motherland.

*

When I began exploring Nigerian history, I found that
it was broken up into three main periods: pre-colonial,
colonial and independent. I began to dig a little deeper,
and was shocked at what I uncovered. I am not sure I
can complete a chapter on identity without some over-
view of Nigerian history, but be warned, this is only
my very basic summary. The Nigeria we know today
was only officially recognised in 1960. Sixty years old!
Nigeria as a nation and as an idea has, however, existed
for millennia. By the eleventh century, the Yoruba
civilisation was established. The Yoruba Empire is
known historically as being based in its original

capital, Ife, but by the seventeenth century Oyo had become the largest Yoruba state. The Hausa-Fulani of the north and the Edo people of Benin were two other tribes that developed major civilisations. Despite all three having minimal power politically, they remained prominent throughout the period of British colonial rule.

The Benin Empire stretched from present-day Lagos all the way east to the Niger Delta, right up until the eighteenth century. However, the onset of colonialism throughout Africa destabilised the continent, allowing the British to expand their unequal trade agreements. It also provided opportunities for them to launch military invasions and, in 1861, Britain captured Lagos.

As these civilisations were turned into a colony, the British imposed treaties so they could take over the trading of resources and minerals. The oil trade at that time was controlled by the British National African Company and, at the Berlin conference of 1884–5, the British were given the rights of influence and control over areas that would later become Nigeria. They used their military superiority to keep power, expand the Lagos Protectorate and establish another in the north. In 1893, the Yoruba Empire entered a treaty which was signed and approved by the Queen mother of Ibadan.

The treaties that allowed the British to maintain control were signed in the 1800s; however, those who agreed to them were not necessarily sufficiently educated in Western politics to understand the consequences, if they had any real choice at all. By the twentieth century, the fight for independence was in motion. Britain had strategic control of the Nigerian people and their resources, but this began to waver in the post-Second World War era as the UK's power declined. Britain's decimated resources, combined with the emergence of an educated Nigerian leadership and a growing clamour for independence, meant that Nigeria finally had a chance to negotiate its future.

The decline of British colonial power coincided with the emergence of a new class of Nigerian political leaders, and a popular nationalist movement. This growing movement, which Nnamdi Azikiwe referred to as an 'African Renaissance' called for Nigerians to unite, develop and take control of their nation. In 1953, there was a transition to independence which was agreed and approved by three regional leaders, Ahamdu Bello from the north, Nnamdi Azikiwe from the east, and Obafemi Awolowo from the west. Eventually, after two revisions, a constitution was approved in 1960 and Nigeria officially became an independent nation on 2 October 1960.

The troubles weren't over yet, though, as regional differences and resource conflicts triggered the Biafran War from 1967–70. Leading up to it in 1966, thousands of Igbo people were killed in ethnic or religious attacks throughout parts of northern Nigeria. Additionally that year, there was a military coup which saw General Yakubu Gowon become the first military leader of Nigeria. In 1967, the east separated from the Republic and the combination of these events sparked civil war. Civilians starved due to ravaged crops and military attacks and, in total, there were an estimated 1 to 3 million casualties.

Learning more about the history of Nigeria made me realise how disconnected I am from the country. I proudly call myself Nigerian and engage with the culture, however I don't necessarily have the same sort of struggle as some of my peers who grew up over there. By looking at Nigeria's colonial history I also came to better understand the reasons many Nigerians have chosen to move away from their home country. Nigeria's colonial past is filled with racism, hate and division. It made me question if I was proud to be British.

*

From Nigeria, I moved on to my best link with the country: my mum. I asked my mum to help me write up a brief history of her life. I realised then that, in all the years I'd been alive, I had never questioned my mum about her past. She told me it's 'difficult to write much about herself', so I suggested we just had a conversation about Nigeria and about what she remembered. What I learned blew my mind.

Mum said that she came from a well-to-do family. Her father, my grandfather, whom I'd never met, was a civil engineer who owned a major property in a 'posh part' of Nigeria's capital Lagos, Ikoyi. Biaduo Street to be exact. The house was beautiful, she said. There was lemongrass growing in the garden and a mango tree reaching up to her bedroom window. She could lift the latch and pick a mango whenever she wanted. The neighbourhood was quiet and peaceful. A wonderful place to grow up. I went on Google Street View to have a look. You can't see much of the house itself, but you can look down the street: gated front gardens, a beautiful tall, blue building, a modern house that looks like it could be a church.

Not counting Britain's dubious role in creating the nation state of Nigeria, my family's link to the mother country goes back quite a way. My grandmother had studied and trained in London as a secretary at what was then named Pitman's College, on Southampton Row, Bloomsbury — the best place to be if you wanted to become a secretary. Upon her return to Nigeria, she pursued a career as a medical secretary in what became a long-term role alongside a cancer specialist named

Professor Kofi Duncan. My grandfather, her husband, was also well educated and spent much of his working life travelling the world as a pharmacist for Wellcome, Glaxo and Pfizer.

Mum's family was big. She labelled her home as 'polygamous', so my grandfather had more than one wife, and seven children in total. My mother was her mother's only child and received as much attention as her siblings (if not more). She was the 'binding cord' connecting everyone and was loved by all. For every child, however, school was of paramount importance, with my mother beginning her studies at the prestigious private nursery Lara Day on the outskirts of Lagos — an institution which prides itself as offering 'an education comparable to the best available in private schools in Africa'.

I asked for more information about my mum's day-to-day life, growing up in Lagos, and was filled with excitement to learn that she had lived near to the greatest Nigerian musician of all time, Fela Anikulapo Kuti, or 'Baba' as she referred to him. For those who don't know him, Fela Kuti is the founder of what is known today as Afrobeat (not Afrobeats), a multi-instrumentalist of world renown, and a pioneering human rights activist. I learned about Afrika Shrine, the club he set up at the Empire Hotel: 'A lot of girls at the time used to just fall in love with Fela. Literally any girl that went missing was said to have eloped to Baba's shrine.' I also heard about Baba the man, not the icon — about his kindness and generosity, about his sidekick, a dog nicknamed Jamba.

My mother was lucky enough to be chauffeured to school until she was about eleven or twelve, when her parents decided that she was old enough to start taking the newly introduced public transport to school. It was a challenge, she remembered, but she quickly adapted, joining the many thousands of Lagos residents grateful for the cheap transport across the capital.

I learned that, for my mother, it was not enough to be good at one thing. You had to excel at everything. Her home life was almost militarily regimented. That aside, mum was the quiet type, so she was perfectly happy to stay in and study or read. Her favourites were Mills & Boon romance novels. She would go through entire series at a time. 'As you might have guessed, there were no boyfriends allowed, so it was my only way to experience romance!' At school, not only was my mum a good runner, she was one of the best in the district. 'I was a class captain, and sports prefect. I participated in the high jump, 100 metre relay and the sprint. I was also a member of the literary and debating society, competing against other prestigious schools. I was even on TV!'

She was pushed at home, but it wasn't only her parents that she had to please: 'School was very, very tough. You couldn't get away with slacking. They had serious disciplinary measures against lateness; for instance, get a cutlass and cut grass until blisters show up on your palms. Next time you know better. You were not even allowed to walk on the grass in case you damaged it. Our uniforms had to be neatly pressed and ironed — no wrinkles. Our socks had to be perfectly white, which was no easy task if you're taking dusty paths to school. The school's motto, which the faculty repeated to you at every opportunity, was supposed to be motivational, but it was more like a warning: "Work is the antidote for poverty." '

With her good grades and academic aptitude, my grandfather pushed my mother towards a career in medicine, the family profession (in a way). Unfortunately, you needed excellent grades in maths to be accepted onto the training course and, sadly, maths wasn't one of Mum's strongest subjects. 'I remember nodding throughout my algebra classes to convince my teacher I understood what she was saying. I didn't have a clue!'

With medicine out the window, Mum decided the next best option would be law. She read up on the profession and found more and more to like. With her passion for reading and outstanding debating skills (not to mention her keen eye for injustice), it seemed like the perfect profession, and the best way to fulfil her old school motto. But it was not an easy path.

*

When I was in my final year, I realised that I couldn't be a doctor, like my father wanted. I just wasn't good enough at maths. You could go straight to university aged sixteen if you managed to get the right grades. I was expected to get the top grades in my class and won a place to study law at a new university that had opened in Lagos. The night before we got our results, however, I had a dream that I got an F in English. It was a horrible dream. The next morning I woke up and went to collect the results and discovered that my dream had come true! No one could believe it! One of the best students in the school, a member of the school debating team, had failed English! I lost my place at university and had to stay on at school for another two years until I got the right grades. Glory be to God, I won a place at a good university outside of Lagos, the University of Benin, and finally left home. I was privileged.

I threw everything I had into my degree. I became vice-president of the Law Student Association [LSA], and travelled around the country, meeting fellow law students. It was during my travels with the university that I first met Chukwuemeka Ojukwu, blessed be his memory, a political leader who played a pivotal role in the Biafran War of the late 1960s, and led the breakaway Republic of Biafra. He became the patron of the LSA, and was someone we spent a bit of time with. He was a very intelligent man, and a very kind man. We got along well. I was sort of the mother of the LSA and would look after everyone, as best I could, and I think he recognised that in me, and gave me encouragement and support when he could.

A lot happened in Nigeria during my youth. I was very lucky to have had a relatively peaceful childhood. My parents paid for me to fly back home regularly, whereas most people had to drive. I would be collected from the airport by our driver and taken home, where I was warmly welcomed and well looked after.

Eventually I graduated and moved on to law school, in Victoria Island. It was a very privileged place. My fellow students were the children of the country's top business people, politicians and artists. Everyone had a lot of money. And everyone liked to party. Our generation was rebellious. I remember my grandmother used to call us 'butter children', because we were so soft. She would give us material to make traditional Nigerian clothes, and we'd make tight trousers and tops. When she saw us, she would go crazy! I had a wonderful time and did well. I was a lawyer. My English wasn't quite good enough for me to have a top job in Lagos maybe, but I was well qualified, and lived a good life.

In my final year of university, I was living in an apartment alone in Victoria Island. I was very good friends with my neighbour from across the hall. We would go to the market together most days. One day we got back from the market and I started cooking up the peppers I had bought, when I heard a scream from across the hall. At first I thought my friend had spilled hot water on herself or something, so I hurried over to see what was going on. Her door was ajar and it was dark inside. I called out her name and walked in. In the living room, my neighbour was kneeling on the floor, surrounded by men with guns. Robbers. One of them grabbed me, threw me on the ground and pressed a gun to my head. They tied us up with rope and started interrogating my friend about what jewellery and money she had in the apartment. My friend was crying uncontrollably. I had no idea what to feel. It was all very surreal, but I thought if I just stayed still and didn't speak we would be OK. And luckily, that's what happened. The robbers completely ransacked the house, and left with a little bag full of money and gold. We waited for a while and then managed to wriggle free, and ran downstairs and into the street. Nobody could believe we had escaped without being hurt. These robbers were ruthless. They would rape and kill without a care in the world. It was God that kept us safe.

Eventually I finished my degree with good marks. I had the world at my feet, but I decided to take a little break before I made a decision about my career. I moved back home and spent a lot of time with my family, with my mother especially. Then all of a sudden, everything changed. A man fell in love with me, a man my older sister knew. Back then, there was no courtship. He asked my father if he could marry me and my father agreed, and that seemed to be that. My parents asked me what I thought, but I knew nothing of love, so I just went along with it. Even though my father approved, it was a strange match. My parents wanted the best for me, but I'm not sure he was really it. He didn't really have a job, but he had big dreams.

So all of a sudden I had a fiancé, but I was still living at home, taking a bit of time off after my degree. I was rest-less. Soon enough my fiancé was offered a job in England and we decided to go. I was very independent, and always have been, so it wasn't much of a step for me. It was excit-ing. I also thought it might be safer than Lagos at that time. My mother told me, 'Don't forget who you are. A good name is better than gold and silver.'

*

Growing up, I had always wondered why my parents, and so many of my friends' parents, had left their home countries to start all over again in Britain. It was another question I never bothered to ask. Looking around at our surroundings, at the relentless grey sky, at the poverty of our neighbourhood, at the lack of opportunities, it was easy to think that they must have come from somewhere far worse. My view was only reinforced by the damaging stereotype that is still propagated: that the entire continent of Africa is full of poor, dirty and hopeless people. As I got older, I began to challenge that view, but it was only when I asked the question that I began to discover why my mother, and why so many people like her, had chosen to move to the UK.

*

The reasons why people move from one country to another are often far from straightforward. I'm not going to provide you with a lesson in human migration here, but I think it's important to look more closely at immigration or, more precisely, at the movement of people to a country where they do not possess citizenship in order to work and take up permanent residence.

In particular, there are a few key myths which are worth dispelling. Firstly, not all immigrants are refugees. In fact, the UN's 2017 international migration report found that only 10 per cent of migrants worldwide are refugees or asylum seekers.

Secondly, migration isn't just about poor people moving to richer countries. Here, the difference between what the tabloids might tell you and the reality is especially stark when it comes to asylum seekers and refugees. In 2015, in the middle of the 'refugee crisis' when millions of people fled the Syrian civil war, Britain's press and even its prime minister spoke about 'swarms' of refugees trying to enter into Britain. However, as of 2018, only 13,000 Syrian refugees had been resettled in Britain, compared to over three million in Turkey and over two million in Lebanon. This isn't just the case with Syrian refugees, and data from the UN shows that of the world's 26 million asylum seekers and refugees, 4 out of 5 are living in the developing world.

In fact, patterns of all kinds of migration are more complex than they might seem. When it comes to so-called 'economic migrants', the UN show that migrants from developing countries are more likely to move to *other* developing countries than they are to move to the world's wealthiest states. In fact, in 2017, of all the world's migrants, 38 per cent were people who were born in developing countries who had moved to *other* developing countries, 35 per cent were people who had moved from developing countries to developed countries, 20 per cent were people who had moved *between* rich countries, and 6 per cent had moved from developed to developing countries. Perhaps most surprisingly, the continent with the fastest growing migrant population is not Europe or North America, but Africa.

Finally, and perhaps most importantly, we should dispel the myth that migrants offer little to their country of arrival. Most research on the subject concludes that migration has, on average, a positive economic effect on receiving countries, not to mention the social and cultural benefits migration brings. What's more, international migration more often than not benefits the countries from which migrants come, as remittances sent back to family can enable development there, and many development economists argue that the best way to reduce poverty globally would be to reduce barriers to labour mobility.

Now we've got that general context out of the way, it's important to get specific. After all, this isn't a textbook about migration, but rather a chapter about how migration has affected *my* identity. And, as a young man with Nigerian parents who moved to Britain, we need to take a look at the specific reasons why people have, over the last seventy years at least, been keen to move to these Isles.

The history of migration to Britain is intimately tied up with the history of Britain and of the British Empire. At its height, Britain controlled a quarter of the world's population and a fifth of its land mass. This was no benevolent role, however; Britain gained its Empire, and maintained it, through coercion, aggression and often appalling acts of violence. Yet in spite of its actions,

Britain was eager to present itself as the 'motherland', immeasurably improving the lives of its colonial subjects, and as a land which would welcome them unreservedly, if they were ever to make the journey across the ocean.

This would become significant at the end of the Second World War. Then, two factors combined to change Britain forever. First, the declining legitimacy of the British Empire meant the British wanted to present the relationship between Britain and its colonial subjects as equals within a commonwealth. Second, the war had left the British economy close to collapse, and the country's attempts to rebuild its infrastructure were plagued by labour shortages. The result was the passing of the 1948 British Nationality Act, which would allow Britain's approximately 800 million subjects around the world to live and work in the UK without need of a visa.

The first big post-war arrival of people to Britain, and still the most famous, was on the *Empire Windrush*, which in June 1948 brought 802 people to Britain from the Caribbean. What followed was a steady stream of economic migrants arriving in the UK from former colonies, rising from 3,000 a year in 1953 to 136,400 in 1961, in spite of a number of increasingly draconian and overtly racist policies and acts passed by successive British governments to limit the number of new arrivals and, in some cases, deport those who had arrived in search of a new life.

While countless articles have been written about the racism within the immigration system ruining lives, there has been much less media attention given to the historical evidence that sits within the public record regarding migration policies, such as the Commonwealth Immigration Act of 1962, which saw the sitting Conservative government introduce measures that restricted the automatic right to remain in the UK for Commonwealth citizens. The government not only limited those permitted to settle in the UK but, in many cases, actively discriminated against those applying to come to the UK from the global south, while paying for the relocation of workers from countries such as Australia and New Zealand. This was later amended by the Immigration Act of 1971 and many times subsequently, but these discriminatory practices have led to the unfair restriction and the detention and wrongful deportation of hard working and rightful citizens of the UK.

*

In 2018, we had a new political scandal that would shake communities across the UK. The so-called Windrush scandal exposed the government's inability to recognise generations of families who journeyed over to the UK from the Caribbean post-Second World War, responding to the call to the Commonwealth to rebuild the 'motherland'; in other words, Britain relied on nations over which they held sovereignty to help the country get back on its feet.

Those who first arrived in the UK were segregated by overt discrimination. When my grandmother came to the UK to study, there were signs in shops and house windows which stated: 'No Blacks, No Irish, No Dogs.' It was fine to call someone coloured or a negro. Racism thrived in this unwelcoming environment. But Britain's hostility didn't stop the thousands of people who wanted to have a better life from arriving in the UK during the fifties and sixties.

New census data showed that 21,000 people who moved to the UK before 1971 have neither a British passport nor a passport from the country where they were born, giving the strongest picture so far of the possible scale of the Windrush scandal. It has even exposed that a number of legal British citizens were separated from their families and sent back home to a country they had not seen since they were children.

Some fifty years on from their arrival, some have been arrested and put in immigration detention centres, others have been forced out of their homes and jobs or denied NHS treatment or benefits.

Today, not much has changed. We see migrants coming to Europe from all parts of Africa, Asia and beyond. For some, their journeys are smoother than others'. The news cycle has made us very aware of the dangers some have faced in order to cross the Mediterranean, but the majority of the economic migrants entering the UK from Nigeria in the nineties and early 2000s saved up and purchased plane tickets to the 'mother country' with hopes of bettering their lives. Although their journeys were not riddled with the same dangers that we have witnessed on the news in recent years, they came with their own hardships. Stories of trained professionals who are unable to gain anything other than menial employment are still all too common in 2020. This is not to say that there is no honour or dignity in these jobs, but in many cases they do not reflect the skill sets or qualifications individuals have worked hard to acquire in their home country. It's a basic point, but it demonstrates the ways in which the trauma of Empire continues to resonate, Britain stopping its own citizens from full access to a society that was built from their countries' contributions.

The Windrush scandal came to light in 2018 following a determined effort by the *Guardian* and a number of activists and writers. I can only imagine how things must have been in 1993 when my mum first came over. She had a long battle to be recognised as a British citizen, even though she came over to contribute to the economy and use her professional skills. The plight of those with an insecure right to live and work in Britain has a particular relevance in the context of Brexit. 3.2 million EU citizens living in the UK who previously had an automatic right to live here will now have to apply for 'settled status', and anyone living in Europe who wants to move to the UK in future will have to jump through the same hoops that my mum had to.

*

My mother was only one of many hundreds of thousands of migrants who made the journey from Nigeria to the UK in search of a different life. She came to make a positive contribution as so many others did, as part of a steady wave of African migrants who came to the UK between 1990 and the early 2000s. According to the Office for National Statistics (ONS), there has been a significant growth in economic immigrants from Nigeria arriving the UK since the early 1990s. If you focus on movement from 2000 to the present in particular, the picture becomes even clearer. Between 2001 and 2002, Nigerians accounted for the fifteenth largest number of migrants settled in the UK. By 2015, Nigerians were the ninth most prolific migrants in Britain, ranking as the second most common sub-Saharan African migrants in the country, just behind South Africa. In 2015 the ONS statistics record 102,000

Nigerian women registered in the UK, compared to 97,000 Nigerian men.

My mother was one of those women.

*

I remember feeling a bit disappointed when I arrived. In Nigeria we didn't always have electricity and the roads were awful, but I wasn't that impressed with London initially. It was mid-February and freezing cold, and a bit dreary. Our house was a lot smaller than our family home in Lagos.

Needless to say, things didn't work out as I hoped they would in London. Things weren't really working out with my partner and I felt very alone. Soon after we arrived, we broke up. I didn't think I could go back to Lagos, so I decided to stay. I foolishly thought that I could find a job as a lawyer without too much trouble. I was well qualified and, as the Nigerian legal system is largely based on the British one, I believed a simple conversion certificate would do. I was wrong. My qualifications were invalid. If I wanted to practise as a lawyer, I would need to start from scratch, which I certainly didn't have the money for. I decided to enrol on a technology course instead, learning Microsoft Office at a college not far from where I was staying. I spent a whole year learning Word. Can you imagine! What a waste of time. But I didn't know what else to do.

I met someone new and moved in with him. The pressure eased off a little. I had two children in quick succession. Then things began to fall apart again. I needed to find a job. I spent a while searching and eventually found a job working the night shift at a currency exchange at Gatwick Airport. I was very proud of myself. But not long after I started I began to feel ill. I was so ill that I couldn't work. I could barely get out of bed. It turned out that I was pregnant again, so that was that.

I don't regret it, but I had to make sacrifices. I had to make some very difficult decisions. I focused on the children. My partner, the father of my children, had a stroke and was not taking care of himself. He stopped working. We were also drifting apart, so eventually, he left and moved back to Nigeria. I was on my own with three small children and no income at all. I went to social services to ask for help, but I couldn't understand what they needed from me. They were not very patient. I had to make do. I found a job with British Telecom and was fortunate enough to have a good network of friends and neighbours nearby to help out at home. But it was hard. We were forced to move a lot and lived in a series of unsuitable houses. I remember being called by Jeremiah's teacher, who said that he was very tired because he'd been kept awake by the noisy plumbing in the house. It was not a good time. I was very stressed and it was having an impact on my health. I had issues with my kidneys and I was not really sleeping. My GP sent me to hospital and they said that I needed to have an operation. I couldn't go through with it. I couldn't risk a major operation. If something happened to me, God forbid, what would become of my children? So I struggled on.

We hadn't heard from my former partner in a long time. He would come back to visit the children occasionally and he would call, but then the calls stopped. One day, I got a call from someone in his family. They told me that he had passed away. We hadn't lived together for a long time, but it hit me hard. I was in shock. It was very hard for the children as well. My oldest son did not cope well.

I was working when I could, but I wasn't making much money. I was also applying to become a British citizen. It was a long and expensive and complicated process, and until my paperwork came through, it meant that my status in Britain was uncertain. And because my status was uncertain, my children's status was uncertain.

*

My mother's qualifications before she left Nigeria for the UK were seen as exceptional. As a fully trained and qualified lawyer, the world really was her oyster. Her degree was supposed to set her up for life, however that was far from being the case when she arrived in the UK. Her qualifications were immediately dismissed and not recognised. Of course, laws in the two different countries vary, yet, with Nigeria's colonial past, many of the laws and legislation in Nigeria were actually steered by the British. I find it upsetting that she was seen as unqualified to go into law even though she had worked hard for years to make her dreams come true.

*

Who am I? Putting this chapter together has helped me learn a wealth of things about myself and my family. Most of what you have read I only learned while writing this book. Knowing who you are is so important. For most of my life I feel I hadn't found myself. I had so many questions about my ancestry, my family history and my mother's story. These answers I have finally found after embarking on this journey.

After learning about what my mum had had to forego, and about her hard work and struggle, it taught me the importance of a strong family unit. I appreciate her even more because of the sacrifices she made. You may be wondering, how do you find yourself? One important way is to discover your roots. After learning about Nigeria and my family's history, it allowed me to feel more connected to myself. When you are more aware about such a basic thing, it can change your entire outlook on life.

Rather than accept who people say you are, find out for yourself. It's an ongoing process for me, and I am still learning more, but I believe my second email to Lord Hastings was not far off. Knowing yourself leads to knowing your purpose. I believe everyone on this earth has a purpose, it's our responsibility to find out why we're here.

2

Home

My family is small. I grew up with my mother and sister and brother. We were often joined by a number of older family friends and relatives – aunties and uncles of all shapes and sizes – but for the most part, it was just us four. When I was very young, I had no idea that our family was in any way unusual or out of the ordinary. It was a series of small moments that made me think otherwise. The day in June when we made Father's Day cards in school and I wasn't sure what to do with mine. Or the fact that it was only my mum who came to parents' evening, when most of my friends had two parents with them. After every Christmas, classmates would ask what my dad got me for Christmas and I would make up stories to hide the fact that he wasn't around.

Or there was the dream. I was eight years old or so at the time, but I still remember every detail. In the dream, I was lying in bed, in the middle of the night, when I heard our front gate squeak. I opened my curtains just in time to see my father walk down our path and up to our front door. There was a gentle knock, the door opened and closed. I could hear him downstairs, moving about, talking to my mum. Laughing. I didn't go down, but there was something about just being in bed, knowing he was there, that gave me a feeling that is very difficult to describe. It was a dream that felt so real that, after I woke up, I spent the next few hours staring out of the same window, looking down the dark street expectantly, waiting for him to arrive. I waited until it became light. Nothing.

Not long afterwards, I remember walking into the house after school to silence. Something seemed off, but I couldn't work out what it was. By the evening, when my mum had still not appeared, I crept up the stairs to her door. I heard the sound of crying from her room. I remember thinking that I should check on her, but as I walked in, she began to wipe her eyes, as if nothing had happened. She wouldn't tell me what was wrong and assured me that everything was alright.

That week, the strange feeling continued. Things weren't quite right. If my brother or sister or I were naughty or loud, my mum wouldn't tell us off like she usually did. She didn't make us go to bed and didn't stop us from watching television. We even managed to watch an episode of *The Simpsons*, a show that was usually forbidden. However, the main thing I noticed was my mother herself. She had changed in some way. Her shield of happiness had disappeared; she was quiet, withdrawn and wouldn't really speak to us.

After school on Thursday, she picked all of us up from school and took us to the park. This was another strange occurrence, but we were over the moon. We ran around in the evening and laughed and jumped on each other, with my mother watching from the park bench. After a while, when we were sweaty, she asked if we would like McDonalds for dinner, or if we wanted to go and play games on the computer in the internet café. We couldn't believe our luck, screaming and shouting with joy. But then she started to cry and knelt down next to us. 'Gather around me and hold each other's hands,' she said. She told us she loved us and cared about us and would be here for us always. 'Your father has passed away.' I remember freezing, holding my breath. Death was not a new concept to me and I fully understood what she meant. To think that the man I had been waiting for had gone for ever was too much for me. It broke my heart into a million pieces.

It is a cliché to say it but in that moment, everything changed. I knew instantly that things would not be the same, that I would have to step up in some way, that I would have to do more. Even at that young age, I accepted the responsibility and made a vow that one day, when I had my own children, I would never ever leave their side.

*

This chapter is called home, but it's really about what home means. A physical structure, but also the people who make a house a home. Family. Throughout my entire life I have been amazed by the strength and courage of my mother. She played the role of two parents within our household. My parents separated when I was four, so I have no memories of them together. Her contribution to my success can never be overlooked, but for a long time I couldn't help but think about the comparisons between myself and friends and peers who had fathers around to help and guide them. I wondered what it would have been like to have a father to help me with particular scenarios. I love my mother unconditionally, but there was a lot I felt I couldn't speak to her about. I just didn't feel comfortable enough and worried that if I did ask her, she would be angry, confused or upset — or wouldn't be able to relate.

I'll try to be a bit more specific. My mum knew nothing about football, for example, and didn't understand why I was so enthusiastic about it. So I never went to the park to kick a ball about, I didn't go to football lessons, I had no football shirts, I never watched highlights on television. Or when I was twelve or thirteen, I had no one to talk to about the changes I was noticing – growing pains, my voice breaking, the feelings I had for my first ever girlfriend. I didn't have an example in my home environment of a good relationship and this meant I didn't know how to make my relationship function well. I couldn't really speak to my friends about it either, in spite of the fact that they were undoubtedly experiencing the same things. It made me feel like I was weird. It made me feel like I was alone. I didn't know what to do, but I knew that I couldn't tell my mum.

I believe that my mother was the saviour of our family. She worked hard to support us and to give us the best childhood possible. I believe that I have absolutely nothing to be ashamed of. I don't believe in the idea of a perfect family. I don't think one exists. But I do think that the way I grew up had some bearing on who I have become. The Education Policy Institute defines disadvantage as 'not only income poverty, but also a lack of social and cultural capital and control over decisions that affect life outcomes'. By social and cultural capital, what they mean is the kind of background knowledge that children from privileged backgrounds enjoy. You might get it by going to the theatre or art galleries, taking overseas holidays, or having the opportunity to take part in various activities organised outside of school. My mum tried to take me to galleries when she could, but we didn't do many of these things when I was young. Not many people in my community did. My mum didn't really have the time or money to be anything other than a disciplinarian. When you read about my housing situation, in particular, you will also see that my family certainly didn't always have control over the decisions that affected our lives.

For a long time I have thought my background shaped my younger years, and the difficulties I had at school. For example, there were occasions when I would get into trouble at school, forget to hand in homework or engage in low-level disruption because I was bored or disinterested. I feel that if I had had someone at home who had time to talk to me or encourage me more, I might have found a different outlet. The research backs me up. The policy institute I mentioned above found that 'on average, disadvantaged pupils are 4.3 months behind in the early years phase, 9.4 months behind in primary school, and 18.4 months behind at Key Stage 4.'

I also realise that I am lucky, in some ways. My parents separated when I was four, but I did get to know my dad. However, having a glimpse of my father made his absence even more noticeable. Following the separation, we saw him less and less. Firstly at home or he would come and take us out. Then at a special centre, for an hour or so at a time, with toys and games and books and lots of other children playing with their fathers. Then phone calls. Two phone calls a year, at my Aunt Harriet's house. Then nothing.

Parents are an important part of any child's home. But beyond the absence of a mum or a dad, what do we mean when we say 'broken home'? What does home really mean? What is the reality of home life for children growing up in deprived areas, like the one I lived in? What about children who don't have a home?

Even though I lived in a single-parent household, my mum ensured that me and my siblings had the best upbringing. She played two roles, that of a father and a mother, and for this I will be forever grateful.

Absent fatherhood can have a detrimental effect on the lives of the kids involved. I do believe that, if me and many of my peers had had father figures in our homes, we would have skipped past many of the mistakes we made as young men. I also feel we would have learned how to control our thoughts, feelings and actions.

*

Deborah

I don't remember our parents separating. I do remember the centre we used to go to though, to see our father. They give you a set time. It could be one hour, it could be two. We'd arrive and be taken down to a big room, with lots of toys and other kids playing with their parents. Dad would come in and we'd get to play with him until our time was up, and then we'd be taken back to Mum. I didn't know what was going on really. I didn't really get it until I was a lot older.

Most of my friends had two parents growing up. You kind of get jealous a little bit, but you can't change your situation. It sort of felt like their families were the norm and our family wasn't. I say that, but I think we also had an advantage. We had other people raising us too. We had other family members and friends helping. Aunty Harriet, Aunty Letitia, Uncle Boniface — they all supported my mum and helped her to raise us.

I remember Mum getting sick too. We were taken by social services into a home, until a family member came to get us. I can't remember who. I don't really remember a lot about that situation. I'm not sure if that's because I was too young or because I've blocked it out. It wasn't a good time.

*

'Homelessness' is a word many of us are disconnected to, but a word I am familiar with. Between the years of 1999, in which I was born, up until 2006, we were frequently homeless. I moved homes at least seven times in those seven years. Each home was different. Each was located in a different area. Some were large, with bedrooms for me and my brother and sister. One had a big garden, I remember. But many were small, dirty and inadequate. One property only had one bedroom for the four of us. Again, as with my family structure, I felt like this was a process that children all over the country were going through. I had no sense that it was exceptional in any way. As I moved from place to place, school to school, most of my new friends had no concept of what was happening. They remained in the same houses, surrounded by the same people, undisturbed, undisrupted. I felt like we were on the run but I didn't know what we were running from. I couldn't paint my room. I couldn't put up posters. We lived out of suitcases a lot of the time. We never knew how long we would be able to stay. As soon as it felt like we were getting settled, like our new house was becoming our home, my mother would share the news that we were moving again.

*

Esther

My citizenship status affected our life in various ways. For example, for reasons I still don't understand, some-how connected to my application, the council suddenly stopped paying our rent. On a Friday night, I finished work, collected the children and got back home to find our landlord waiting for us in our flat. He said that the rent hadn't been paid and told us to leave. I couldn't believe it. I said, 'Where am I going to go at this time on a Friday night with three small children? I have nowhere to go.' He didn't care. I said, 'My God will keep me here.' The landlord replied, 'Your God is push-ing you out.' I took the children and went to our church. The congregation rallied around us. Thank God for the church. They gave us so much during those years. Food, clothes, places to sleep when we really needed it. Even the use of a car. By Monday, the council had found us a new home not far away, but it was not permanent. For the next few years we were moved from place to place. We were homeless. We always had a roof over our heads, but we lost a lot: furniture, clothes, cooking utensils.

This is not a sad story. We were very lucky indeed. We had lots of good people around us and we made it through. It made us stronger. I have always tried to help

people as much as we were helped. I believe in our com-
munity. I try to give back as much as I can.

*

I guess there were some positives. I got used to adapting quickly to new and sometimes difficult environments. It's a trait that I still possess today and is a lot of help. I'm rarely flustered when things change unexpectedly. I'm not particularly bothered by talking in public or voicing my opinion in meetings. I learned how to be comfortable when I was feeling anything but. That said, it was mostly bad. Looking back, I think I lost a lot of my childhood by moving around so much.

I was never able to settle. This resulted in me not making many friends at that time, not connecting to the community around us, not knowing anything much about our local area. I was always in the house. The only times I would leave were to go to school, to church or to follow my mum to the local youth centres, where she occasionally worked. Looking back, I guess this was also part of my mum's quest to protect us as kids.

We all know that there is a housing crisis in the UK. A recent research project conducted by the National Housing Federation states that an estimated 8.4 million people in the UK are living in unaffordable, insecure or unsuitable homes. That's approximately 15 per cent of the total population. Let's step back a bit. What does that mean? Whose fault is it? According to the website for the Office of the United Nations High Commissioner for Human Rights, housing is:

> the basis of stability and security for an individual or family. The centre of our social, emotional and sometimes economic lives, a home should be a sanctuary; a place to live in peace, security and dignity.

> Increasingly viewed as a commodity, housing is most importantly a human right. Under international law, to be *adequately* housed means having secure tenure — not having to worry about being evicted or having your home or lands taken away. It means living somewhere that is in keeping with your culture, and having access to appropriate services, schools, and employment.

That is pretty clear cut. If housing is unaffordable, insecure or unsuitable, a person's human right to a safe home is not being met. This is a right that should be protected at government level, through suitable policies and programmes, as well as national housing strategies. *No one* should be forced to live in inadequate housing. Yet the numbers speak for themselves.

Not long ago, I came across an even more shocking statistic. Over 200,000 children and families are currently homeless in the UK. This is not homelessness as you might picture it – people in sleeping bags on the street, begging for money – but someone without a permanent residence. It's a kind of invisible or hidden homelessness. The kind of homelessness that afflicted my childhood. In December 2019, a *Guardian* report by Mattha Busby on recent government figures concluded that:

Almost 130,000 children dependent on their parents and carers live in temporary accommodation, across more than 60,000 of the households without permanent homes. More than 7,000 of these are in bed and breakfasts, up 3.2% from the same time last year. At the end of June 2019, there were 13,450 households in temporary accommodation with shared facilities, widely considered the worst type of housing. This has increased by 40% in five years. More than a quarter of these households have been accommodated in different local authority areas, with a large majority of these out-of-district placements from London councils.

I dug a little deeper and was appalled by the scale of the problem. Children growing up in hostels; survivors of domestic abuse forced to sofa surf; families being housed in shipping containers. Shipping containers! What would it be like to live in a shipping container? Residents complained that they were small, noisy and awkwardly configured. Boiling hot in summer and ice cold in winter. Better than being on the streets maybe, but, for a young family, no place to live.

This is an ongoing issue that has been mostly hidden from the public eye, until now. It needs to be discussed. I know, because I was one of those 130,000 children.

*

Deborah

We lived in around six different houses growing up, I think. Crystal Palace, Hawkshaw Close, Kings Avenue, Herne Hill, Gipsy Hill and Brixton. It was long. Scary at times. Usually in life, you do not move as many times as we did when we were young. We didn't have a steady life. I lost contact with a lot of people, a lot of friends. You might meet someone you like one day and move the next. Making friends is a long process. It takes time to build up trust and shared experiences. Imagine what it's like being the new kid in school, again and again. You don't know if people are going to like you. You've got to go through the whole thing again. It's easy to become a victim. It's easy to fall prey to bullies. It was scary. You don't know what's in front of you. You don't know what to expect. You don't know what the future holds.

The reasons why we moved were never really discussed. I don't think I was ever told why we were moving. We would just wake up one morning in a house we'd lived in for a couple of months or a couple of years, and be told to get up and pack. As a child, there was sadness and anxiety, but also a little bit of excitement. You were moving somewhere new! It could be a big house. Or you could be cramped together in one bedroom in a small flat. That happened. We were all in one room. There was actually only one bed, I think. You'd always hope for the best, however. And sometimes it was a nicer house. There was one house with three floors and a big garden, and I had my own bedroom. That was good. I was grateful to have my own bedroom, as the only girl. I could finally have friends over!

It's a sad situation for anyone to be in. With the right support, anything is possible. It's ridiculous that families still have to endure what we went through.

I don't think many people really understand what homelessness is. There are many different types of homelessness. There's the type people will immediately think of: people living on the street, sleeping on cardboard, having to ask for money to get a meal or a cup of tea. There's also hidden homelessness. Someone could not have a home, but be relying on the kindness and hospitality of friends or family, sleeping on sofas or in spare rooms. Temporary accommodation is another form of homelessness and is just as bad as the others, I think. You could be a single parent with a young child and be placed in a one-bedroom flat one day, but moved to a hostel the next. Sharing a bathroom, sharing a kitchen. It's not nice. No stability and no choice.

If you are homeless, you need to contact the borough you live in to apply for help. You submit an application and the borough decides whether you are homeless or not. It's a long and stressful process. I've been on the list for three years and I have a toddler. I know people who have been on the waiting list for five or ten years. There is not enough social housing. Private companies or individuals can buy up social housing and charge a lot in rent. In Elephant and Castle, they demolished the Heygate Estate. Those residents who were forced out may not be able to move back. They won't be able to afford to. Home is more than a property, you know. It's the area you live in, the area you are connected to. It's not fair that some people can be moved around like that.

*

Why did I live such an unusual childhood? How common is an experience like mine? What does it do to children? And what can be done about it?

I still know there are young people out there just like myself. In the exact same position I was in. You feel neglected, restless and have a heart filled with uncertainty. I hope one day this country will ensure that homelessness no longer exists for families and children like myself, and also those who are on the streets with nowhere to go. I have seen many critics on social media argue that many people who have found themselves in a situation such as mine could just 'work harder', 'get a job'; they believe that anyone can get themselves out of this problem. But from my direct personal experience I can say to them, it is not as easy as you think it is.

I had many opportunities taken away from me because my mum was not in the position to support me financially. This definitely affected me within school.

*

Poverty is not one big problem, but lots of little ones. Lots of little difficulties, stresses and fears, all combined. You don't take everything in when you're young, but there were a few moments that stood out.

School was one of the biggest eye-openers for me. Every year, for example, most of my classmates would have a new full set of school uniform. This was something my mum could not afford. I tried my best to hide it. When my mum could afford new bits she would get them in a larger size so they could last for as long as possible. I used to love playing football in the playground; this would often result in my school shoes being damaged, from holes in different parts of the shoe to the sole becoming loose. I had to work my way around it by using glue or repainting my shoes with a marker pen.

I wasn't the best at football, but, like every young boy my age, wanted to become the next David Beckham. Unfortunately, my mum couldn't afford to buy me football boots and the equipment needed. I also couldn't attend some of the sessions my friends did as we couldn't afford the fees. My hopes and dreams of being a footballer were crushed.

Social divides definitely have an impact on how successful an individual can become. If my mum could have afforded extra-curricular activities, a tutor, football coaching sessions – the list goes on – maybe life would have been different.

*

Deborah

There was a children's charity in Croydon that used to hand out Christmas presents and food, I remember. That was nice. They made you feel special. We didn't really get Christmas presents.

I remember my primary school used to have book sales every once in a while; they'd set out the new books on tables in the hall and kids could go in with their parents and buy some. But we never went. We could never afford to get anything and I used to find it so upsetting. I couldn't understand why all the other kids got to buy new books, and I couldn't. I used to love reading. Tracy Beaker, Noughts and Crosses. *And all of these books were brand new! I would be the first person to read them. They would be mine. So one day, before a book sale, I stole some money from mum, from the place where she used to hide it, and went to the sale and bought a load of books for myself. Mum found out, obviously, and I got in so much trouble. She made me return all the books to get her money back, and I had to apologise to the school for stealing. I never forgot that. I understand why now, of course. She was doing so much, and doing the job of a mother and a father.*

It was always little things. Like sports day. There was no school dinner on sports day, so everyone had to bring a packed lunch. It was a special day and everyone had these wonderful packed lunches: crisps, chocolate, cakes, sweets and all sorts of drinks. There was also a shop in the corner of the playing field where you could buy extra supplies. It was a feast. But we just had a sandwich and maybe a yoghurt. We didn't have any money to buy anything else.

Or the fact that everyone had a new haircut, new shoes or new bags at the start of the year, after the summer holidays. Or even just a new uniform. But we couldn't always afford new uniforms. We couldn't afford new shoes or bags. Or school trips. I remember one year we had a school trip to Germany and Mum couldn't afford to send me. She borrowed money from a family member in the end, I think, but it was awful. It was embarrassing.

I used to look at my friends and think, Why can't I have that lifestyle? It's made me more motivated in many ways. To finish my education, to achieve my goals, to make sure I don't find myself in that position again.

The advice I would give to anyone experiencing what we went through is don't give up. You won't be in this situation for ever. It doesn't define you. And if you're ever feeling low, find someone you trust to speak to. It helps more than you think.

*

When I was a little older, I was lucky enough to win a place to study at the Jonas Foundation, a weekend music school in Elephant and Castle. They provided so many opportunities for me when I was a kid. I could learn to play any musical instrument I wanted (I couldn't decide, so I learned four) and how to read sheet music. I was a member of the choir and sang soprano. We entered a number of different competitions, from the BBC's *Choir of the Year* to Sky One's *Must Be the Music*. We even got to travel to Switzerland to sing on trips sponsored by the school's founders.

I was very lucky to have the opportunity to attend the music school. It wasn't an opportunity many people from my community had and for this I was very grateful. I had, by this point, a strong friendship circle and we all had targets to try and achieve grade eight in all of our instruments, which was the highest level. I have memories of creating my own songs with my brother Elijah and his friends Henry and Winfred, who also came to my secondary school. We used to have drum-offs with the African drums and create mash-ups to popular songs on the piano. Music theory was not my forte; I loved to try and find tunes on the piano after I listened to them. I became really good at this and found myself being able to play songs on the piano I had only heard once or twice. Chanel and Diane led the choir, I loved to sing. I was very shy but, when it came to singing, I was so confident. I once thought I would become a professional singer one day. One thing I loved is that all of us who attended were fully focused and music took us away from getting involved with the wrong crowds or surrounding ourselves with the wrong people.

One of the activities that I enjoyed most at the music school was visiting intensive care units in London hospitals at Christmas. We would mainly visit the Royal

Brompton Hospital in Chelsea. Every time we would visit the hospital, my brother, sister and I would take the 345 bus, setting off in Brixton, in the area we had come to settle in, then through Clapham, eventually entering the Borough of Kensington and Chelsea. The first time, I remember looking around as we reached our destination and feeling like I was in another world. There was no litter on the ground, there wasn't an estate block in sight, the pavement looked as if it had been freshly scrubbed. There were super cars, massive houses. It was a side of London I had never experienced before. Not only did it show me how hard I had to work in life, but it reinforced the fact that I had to find ways to overcome all of the things that were holding me back.

As a child this awakening was very important. Not only did it show me how hard I had to work in life, but it reinforced the fact that I was born into the life I lived and I had to find ways to adapt to overcome all of the things that were holding me back. In 2018, the Equality Trust found that households in the bottom 20 per cent of the population had on average a disposable annual income of £12,798. This is such a shocking figure and representative of the growing divide in British society.

As I grew older I came to realise what that bus journey demonstrated and how split our society is. We are broken down into different enclaves within one city. Poverty meets wealth in plain sight. I always thought it funny how you can walk between two different worlds within five minutes. A council estate sitting alongside private roads and giant detached houses. The one thing that I was alarmed about was the fact that people from either side never engaged with each other. I had never met anyone my age who came from that other side, neither did my friends. There was a stark realisation of the very few times we would engage with people from middle- or upper-class backgrounds. Getting into Oxbridge or a Russell Group university maybe. Your manager at work. Or, for many from where I'm from, facing a judge in the courtroom who, highly likely, would have never experienced any of the issues that might have led you into that position.

It is hard to overstate the levels of inequality that afflict London, the city in which I was born. While to any visitor, parts of London exude an image enormous wealth, the Trust for London has shown that one in four Londoners live below the poverty line, a figure worse than the national average. What's more, this has nothing to do with people being unemployed, as the media might have you believe. In fact, the majority of people in poverty in London (like in the rest of the country) live, like I did, in a working family.

How divided the city is, and the consequences of those divisions, were never more apparent than on the night of 13 June 2017.

*

The Grenfell Tower fire will forever haunt me. I remember waking up in the middle of the night to breaking news alerts on my phone. I switched on my laptop and saw photographs of the tower on fire. Previously that day, I'd had an argument with a friend named Chey from college. We had fallen out and hadn't sorted out our disagreements. I knew that Chey lived in the area. I couldn't remember the name of her block, but I recognised the view from all the times we'd FaceTime each other while she was standing on her balcony. I called her phone and it went to voicemail. I called a few more times and still no connection. Fear came over me as I realised that she could potentially live in that tower block. I stayed awake through the night and into the morning, watching as the fire took over the whole structure.

What has also stayed with me is the sight of individuals waving their T-shirts from the windows. I couldn't stop thinking about the residents; what about those that lived on the upper floors?

Early in the morning, I received a message from Chey. She lived close to the tower and had been evacuated, but she was OK. She knew people who lived inside the block, however, and was still waiting for news.

The issue of adequate housing has never been as prominent or as urgent as it was after the fire in which a reported seventy-two people lost their lives. It was the most catastrophic residential fire in the UK since the Second World War. It was also avoidable. The fire, which started in a single flat, was able to spread to the whole building because a year earlier flammable cladding had been fitted to the building, in part to make the building look more attractive to those in the surrounding area. The decision to use cheaper, nonfire retardant cladding would ultimately cost lives.

One of the things I find most outrageous about the tragedy at Grenfell is that local residents had complained beforehand that the building was not safe. For years a group of concerned residents had complained to their landlords – the Kensington and Chelsea Tenant Management Organisation (KCTMO) – and been ignored. This is what Grenfell Action Group wrote on a blogpost in November 2016:

'It is a truly terrifying thought but the Grenfell Action Group firmly believe that only a catastrophic event will expose the ineptitude and incompetence of our landlord, the KCTMO, and bring an end to the dangerous living conditions and neglect of health and safety legislation that they inflict upon their tenants and leaseholders . . . Unfortunately, the Grenfell Action Group have reached the conclusion that only an incident that results in serious loss of life of KCTMO residents will allow the external scrutiny to occur that will shine a light on the practices that characterise the malign governance of this non-functioning organisation. It is our conviction that a serious fire in a tower block or similar high density residential property is the most likely reason that those who wield power at the KCTMO will be found out and brought to justice!'

Those words haunt me. That people living in Grenfell had predicted the tragedy that would cost so many of their lives is truly shocking. It is also hard to think that they would have been similarly ignored if the people who lived there were wealthy as opposed to being poor, many of them migrants. Grenfell residents died in their homes because of ineptitude from their landlords, and because they were the type of people that those with power in Britain find it easy to ignore.

It is difficult to know what the legacy of Grenfell will be. For a while, it seemed like the tragedy would be a wake-up call for the country, shining a light on inequality so that it could be addressed. But the tragedy seems to have fallen from public attention with little having changed. There are still a number of tower blocks in the UK with the exact same cladding years on; this issue still has not been resolved.

It is also too soon to know whether, like the Grenfell Action Group predicted, those responsible for the tragedy will be brought to justice. The second part of the Grenfell Inquiry, which will look at who is to blame for installing unsafe cladding and other failures might not report until 2022, five years after the fire.

Finally, we also cannot separate the discussion of Grenfell from our earlier one about migration and citizen rights. Many of the Grenfell residents were undocumented, not listed on tenancy agreements and home sharing. In the aftermath of the fire, debates raged as to the number of lives lost. Volunteers and charities working for the support effort reported a number of undocumented migrants and illegal tenants who had lost everything in the fire but were too afraid to come forward. Sadiq Khan, the mayor of London, publicly called on the government for an amnesty to ensure that any illegal immigrants who were victims of the blaze were protected. At the back of my mind I couldn't help but wonder if there were other names missing from the list of the dead. What about the 'hidden homeless' housed in the upper floors?

*

The tragedy at Grenfell is just the most extreme example of a crisis that is far more widespread. In one of the wealthiest societies in the world I find it mind-blowing that so many people are denied adequate housing.

A main reason for this is the decline in new social housing being built over the last thirty years. In the 1970s, 150,000 social homes were built a year. By the 1990s this had fallen to 30,000 and in the 2000s to 25,000 per year. At the same time, over a million council homes were sold to their tenants. This might have been helpful for the people who bought the homes, but because they weren't replaced it meant people like my family were stuck on long council waiting lists, without a secure home.

It is also one of the reasons my generation will struggle to settle down. A recent report from the right-leaning think tank Civitas showed that in 2017 more than one in four people aged 20 to 34 still live with their parents, a rise from less than 20 per cent two decades earlier. It's hard to disagree with Liz Emerson, Co-founder of the Intergenerational Trust, who, responding to the report, told the *Guardian* that 'for young people this means a loss of independence and shattered dreams and reflects that the older generation own more than their fair share of housing wealth'. Finally, someone from the older generation who recognises that the problems of people my age aren't because we're 'snowflakes', but because we're getting a raw deal!

Yet whilst the housing crisis can be expected to affect almost everyone from my age group, the statistics that hit me the hardest are the ones on hidden homeless-ness. Homelessness is poorly understood by many in society, who assume someone is only homeless if they are living on the street. However, as Shelter points out, homeslessness isn't just a question of whether you are sleeping rough, but whether or not you have a home. If you are living in temporary accommodation or on a friend's couch, you may have a roof over your head, but that doesn't mean you have a home.

Shelter have estimated that 320,000 people in Britain are currently homeless. I know what that feels like, because my family was one of those.

When we lived in temporary accommodation, we knew we could be moved at any moment. I remember being in some houses for only a few weeks, before being moved on once again. That meant not being able to blink before I found myself in a completely different space. They say home is where the heart is. I had a family, but I had nowhere to call home until I was seven years old.

Whilst I cannot overlook the hard work of those within the local authority who ensured a family like mine would not find themselves on the street, I cannot help but blame the government for the situation my family found itself in. It is shocking to me that in one of the wealthiest countries in the world we cannot guarantee a secure home for everyone who lives here. It is a basic human right.

I believe every child and family in this country should have a right to adequate housing, and that the government can do more to identify and support those who have found themselves in this situation. For far too long they have relied on the third sector to find solutions to the problems they have partly caused.

It also seems clear what the solution should be, even if it cannot be achieved over night. Shelter have themselves estimated that three million social houses need to be built to secure adequate housing for people in this country. That is a large figure, but it is doable, and it is only making up for the inaction on the part of governments that went before. As Polly Neate, the Chief Executive of Shelter has said, solving the housing crisis 'requires bold action' but 'the cost of not acting is far greater'. The costs will include more hardship and missed opportunities for people with childhoods like mine.

Finally, and I should be clear, I know I am not the only person out there that has been affected by this issue. I know there are many children and families who are experiencing the same thing right now. All I can say to those who are experiencing what we experienced is don't give up. You will find a way out of your situation. And if you are lucky enough to have a roof over your head and a stable income, try to help. Educate yourself about the housing crisis and homelessness in the UK. Support local food banks and organisations such as Crisis and Shelter. Be alert to the signs that someone you know is in trouble. And if they are in trouble, do all you can to get them the help and support that they need.

3

Education

One afternoon when I was doing a bit of research for this chapter, I came across an interview with a Cambridge professor named Diane Reay. The eldest of eight children, Reay grew up on a council estate and received free school meals. After a twenty-year career in teaching, she became a faculty member of one of the most elite academic institutions in the world. Reay experienced the class divide that still shapes our nation from both sides. In the interview, she says it's a common idea that the English state school system provides roughly the same education for all. It's an idea, she says, that is simply not true. 'The most important thing

I found out was that we are still educating different social classes for different functions in society.

I felt that, within my own school experiences, I wasn't encouraged to thrive. Success always had its limits and anything above this was deemed as being too over-ambitious or unrealistic. I always had a question on my mind. I always felt like me and my friends, all from working-class backgrounds, were trained to work *for people*. A much smaller proportion of the population are trained to have people work *for them*.

Over the last fifty years we have seen dramatic improve-ments in many sectors of British society. One thing has remained resolutely the same. Inequality in the educa-tion system. This chapter explores why that inequality persists and what it can lead to.

*

I realise how this is going to make me sound, but I always enjoyed school, even if I struggled to concen-trate sometimes. I guess it was my escape from the issues we were facing at home. It was a great way to make friends, network and (most importantly kids!) learn. I learned so much — from the curriculum, from teachers, but also from school itself. Some of my great-est life experiences happened within school. I don't think at the time I truly understood the importance of school and the impact it would have on making me the individual I am today.

I can't think all the way back to when I started primary school, but I do remember it being a loving and safe environment. Even though we moved house a lot, my mum always ensured me and my siblings stayed put at the same primary school. Her main reasoning behind this was to ensure we had the least disruption possible.

I attended Christ Church primary school in Streatham, south London. The uniform consisted of grey trousers, a white shirt (or collared T-shirt), a grey cardigan with the school's logo embroidered on the right-hand side, grey trousers and a black, white and red tie. There's a school photo of me from when I was six or seven, smiling in that awkward way you do in school photos. I look so neat. For some reason, I always made an effort to look sharp, even though we couldn't afford to regularly buy new school uniforms every year. Maybe it was my way of establishing my identity.

Christ Church was a Church of England school, and it was a good school. I had been going to church with my mum since I was a baby, so the prayers and hymns in assembly were familiar to me, even comforting. There was only one class per year group, so everyone knew each other; the teachers were supportive and kind, and I had a strong group of friends. School was a kind of sanctuary. As I said in the previous chapter, I moved seven times before I was eight, but no matter where we moved to, my mum kept me in Christ Church. What this meant was that I sometimes had a very long journey. One house was so far away that I had to leave the house at 7.30 a.m. with my mum to make sure I arrived on time. In those first years, there was a lot of stress at home. My mum didn't have enough time to help me with my homework or my reading, and I started to struggle. In fact, I was doing so badly that the school thought that I might have special educational needs. I started to have regular meetings with the special needs coordinator and lessons in a small group until I caught up. I remember thinking that it was unfair; that I was just falling behind, not unable to do the work. After a couple of months I was formally assessed and they realised they'd made a mistake, after which I made sure I tried a bit harder in the classroom.

The school helped out in other ways. They let my mum use the washing machine in the staff room to wash our clothes when we didn't have a washing machine at home and, in one particularly bad house with no hot water, they let my brother take a shower before school (my mum made me take cold baths). It wasn't easy. I was a bit of a clumsy child and used to bump my head a lot, prompting a visit to the school nurse and a call to my mum (they would always call if you banged your head). Looking back, I wonder if part of that was seeking attention — seeking the attention I maybe wasn't getting at home.

I was from a low-income family. In theory, this should have had profound implications on my performance at school. A 2019 survey by the National Education Union (NEU) of 8,600 school leaders, teachers and support staff paints a bleak picture of the academic prospects of children living in poverty. Nine out of ten people who took part in the survey agreed that poverty and low income were having a negative effect on pupils' education. Half stated the situation had worsened over the last three years. The survey also concluded that budget cuts were having a significant impact on the ability of some schools to counter the effects of poverty, with breakfast clubs being forced to close due to budget cuts and staff spending their own money on clothes for pupils. The NEU survey really made me think. It described children hiding in the toilets on packed-lunch days because they were so ashamed of their lunches, and children being brought in to school when they were ill because their parents couldn't afford to take time off work to care for them.

I remember that my mum wasn't always able to take us to school or collect us. There were quite a few occasions when one of her friends would appear unexpectedly at the school gates to take us home. She couldn't afford childcare, so after school my older brother and sister used to look after me a lot of the time, even though they were only a couple of years older than me. It was the best my mum could do in the circumstances. You've got to remember that not only was she having to work every hour she could to support us but, as I described in Chapter 1, she was also battling for her right (and ours) to stay in the UK.

I enjoyed most subjects, but I *loved* PE. Loved it. Football especially, but I also was really good at rounders, hockey and patball (if you know, you know). Being outside, socialising and working with my team mates (or on my own, in the case of patball) was another important part of my early school life. Living so far from school and so far from my friends, for the first few years of my education at least, meant that I didn't really have the opportunity to play or develop the kinds of skills and confidence that sports can encourage. I didn't go to any sports clubs outside of school and my mum didn't have the time or energy to play with me. PE might seem like a less-important subject to some, but it definitely helped to build up my confidence, my problem-solving skills, and taught me how to work as part of a team. It also helped to develop a strong competitive streak in me. It's one thing playing well, but it's another to win . . .

Another welcome lesson was IT, where I learned how to code. It sparked a lifelong interest in computers and technology (so much so that I took my IT GCSE early). I'm still obsessed with Python.

My favourite teacher was Ms Baker. She always had time for me. If there were any subjects or topics that I struggled to grasp, she would sit down with me and go through the work until I understood it. She had the ability to make sense of everything. I was lucky. Nearly every teacher at primary school went out of their way to help me and make me feel supported, encouraged and able. No one ever doubted my potential or put me down. I really can't begin to explain what that meant or how important it was to my future successes. Because people believed in me from a very young age, I believed in myself. I was also lucky, because my teachers really didn't have the time or resources to help me in the way they did. In another recent survey carried out by the NEU, 69 per cent of primary and more than half of secondary teachers described their workload as 'unmanageable'. Only 67 per cent of newly qualified teachers stay in the profession for more than three years. In inner-city primary schools, with potentially higher numbers of pupils with English as an additional language, more students with additional needs and greater numbers on free school meals, it is no easy task to ensure that every child gets the attention he or she deserves. This is especially true at a moment when primary schools are seeing their budgets being cut dramatically. A *Guardian* investigation in

March 2019 revealed 'a system falling apart at the seams', with teachers doing the work of canteen staff and cleaners, relying on parent donations for essential funds, and lacking the resources to properly help those pupils most in need. Again, it is important to say that I was lucky in attending a school that went above and beyond to make sure that my every academic need was met and more. What about the many children across the country who are not as fortunate as I was?

*

Einstein once said, 'Everybody is a genius. But if you judge a fish by its ability to climb a tree, it will live its whole life thinking it's stupid.' You may wonder what I'm talking about. Just remember that you can't expect a fish to climb a tree. By year six, I wasn't one of the brightest pupils necessarily, but I was definitely one of the most enthusiastic. For me, getting good grades was a priority. I was predicted reasonably good results for my SATs and did a lot better than expected.

My good results motivated me to do more. They reinforced my passion for school, they gave me additional confidence, they encouraged me to invest more time and energy in my schoolwork and my extra-curricular activities. This may sound as if I'm making a lot of a test that doesn't really mean a great deal, on the surface at least, but it did. It was a measure of our ability. Because of my SATs results, when I started secondary school, I was put in the top set in every class. I was aiming for top marks. No one, at the start of secondary school at least, believed that I couldn't achieve that goal. But what does it mean if you struggle with tests? What does it mean if your strengths lie in other areas? Even as a young child, I felt that it was an unfair way of measuring the ability of a child. Aged ten, I could see that it was a system that benefitted those in my class who were good at taking tests, regardless of their literacy and numeracy skills, but put my friends who weren't as good at retaining information or focusing for long periods at a particular disadvantage. I was lucky, but who lost out? In a 2018 National Education Union survey, nine in ten teachers agreed that SATs are detrimental to children's wellbeing. This is an exceptionally high number. If almost every teacher feels this way, what about their pupils? What about those children whose future academic careers are shaped at that early stage? The fish who can't climb?

Part of the problem in having a system so focused on academic results is that there is very little room for experiences or ambitions beyond those results. Irrespective of how well they fare in tests, 49 per cent of young people feel that they are unprepared for the world of work by the time they leave school. Businesses also agree; they report that 90 per cent of school leavers and a staggering 50 per cent of graduates are not ready for employment.

So if everyone seems to agree that our system isn't working, then why isn't it being changed? If pupils in primary schools are feeling the pressure, what does it mean for children as they get older?

*

Secondary school was finally a time to become more independent. Growing up in primary school, this was the pinnacle of all of our hard work and the end goal. Something that we all dreamed about. My primary school was fairly small but secondary school was an entirely new environment, with hundreds of students, different year groups and harder qualifications. Secondary was supposed to set you up for your future. My brother went to a school called Archbishop Tenison's, located in Kennington directly across from the Oval cricket ground. He would always tell me about the cricket matches and how every single student had a free ticket — from looking out of the third-floor windows. An all-boys' school was something new to me, as primary school had been mixed, with both girls and boys in each class. However, it was a new prospect to be around boys only for the next five years. I knew about

Archbishop Tenison's because it was seen as cool to go there. Everyone used to speak about that school. It was a goal for many students to get a place there. If you made it through the full five years, you would become something called a 'Tenisonian'.

A Tenisonian is someone who is a member of the alumni or an ex-student. I was looking forward to entering this big environment, but I was also anxious. I had never experienced bigger facilities, bigger space and being around new people. From reception to year six, I had only known my primary school. Now many of my friends would go to other schools and only one person followed me to mine. This was a new beginning. When my mum made up her mind about something it could never be changed, so I had no choice but to attend Tenison's, even though there were a few other options that I would have liked to explore. I remember my first open evening, going along to the school and meeting many of my brother's teachers. I knew loads of his friends already and I was looking forward to joining the school. He was only two years above me, so we would spend three years in the same school together. My first day was exciting. I was looking forward to a new beginning, wearing my newly bought school uniform.

I couldn't wait to have my first ever lesson. And we had a range of new subjects that we would learn. Which I was most excited about! I remember walking through the school gates on the first day and it was only us brand-new year sevens who were in the school. The school was massive. My little primary school didn't come close. This was a new level. A multi-storey building, loads of different classrooms, a massive playground. This would be a new environment. The second day was the most challenging. Now we were joined by the rest of the school. I had never been in such a busy environment. Hundreds of people walking around. I was fortunate enough to have known a few young people who had joined me in my year group, even though they didn't attend my primary school. Mikes, Tosin and Jesse were three people I knew through church and mutual friends. I was so happy that they were in the same school as me. I had also bumped into a few people that I'd known growing up in my area; it was good that we were now in the same place. Now students at Tenison's. My secondary school was a Church of England school, the same as my primary school.

This meant that Christianity was at the heart of every-thing we did in school. The same thing happened. Singing hymns in assemblies at the beginning. Hearing a few words from Father Robert. And learning about really important life lessons alongside Christian teachings. I felt that even though our school was multicultural, with stu-dents of many different faiths, the Christian foundation of the school provided a structure and a discipline that really helped us. This was definitely something to pull all of us together with everyone participating.

Travelling was also different now. Rather than walking round the corner back to my home, which was located just behind the playground of my former school, less than a one minute walk away, now I had to commute to school. I would jump on a bus all the way towards Brixton, then down Brixton Road until I reached Kennington. This was new to me. A sense of independence, a sense of confidence now began to grow within me. I used to take different routes to school, depending on which friend I met up with in the morning. We saw so many things on our journey to school. First we saw all of the other students from the neighbouring secondary schools. We saw people rushing to get to work.

But I had to always ensure that I got to school on time, An 8.30 a.m. start to be precise, in order to have a successful school day. My head teacher was Mrs Sims, a female headmistress of an all-boys' school. She was the greatest head teacher I have ever experienced in my whole life. Her dedication to really impact the lives of all the young boys who attended the school was paramount. I was glad she was our head teacher. I later formed a strong, close bond and very good relationship with her, as the years went by in school. However, at the beginning, when I first joined the school, I definitely feared bumping into her in the corridor and was really scared to approach her with any concerns that I had. However, as I started engaging with extra-curricular activities, it became a regular occurrence that we would have meetings and sit down to talk about all of the work I was involved with. I would say that Tenison's was a hard-core school. If you went to Tenison's, you had to be brave and bold, and if you managed to get through five years of that school it was an achievement. Many people were given permanent exclusions or left the school for personal reasons. You might be wondering, what do I mean by hard-core?

Well, let me paint a picture for you. My school was located in Kennington. Very close to Vauxhall, but also very close to Camberwell, Brixton, Stockwell and Wandsworth. We had students from all different parts of London who attended the school, and therefore young people from areas plagued with gang rivalry. Our school connected all of these areas together. And as you can imagine, sometimes it wasn't the best thing for business. I would often come across young men who would fall into disagreements or who would have arguments. But the majority would leave any tensions at the school gates. One thing I noticed is that many of the young men who went to school with me had experienced some of the problems that I had to face growing up, from absent parents to being in the care system, as well as some being young carers at home. Many people were really living in poverty. For the first time, I felt like I could relate nearly to everyone around me.

As we settled into school, I started to realise that there were two things that everyone cared about: money and girls. Being in an all-boys' school and growing up, there were many different social pressures. The older boys in our school created the framework we would follow. They would meet up with girls from Charles Edward Brooke and St Martin-in-the-Fields, which were both all-girls' schools. We would watch as they came to school in designer outfits, wearing the newest clothes; some wore trainers and brought their own designer bags to school. This now became the thing everyone wanted; you wanted to be like the popular guys. These social pressures often led to people doing things they shouldn't have to create this image — some guys I knew started engaging in criminality in order to fund their lifestyle.

My first two years were the most eventful. I got involved in as many extra-curricular activities as possible. The school choir, basketball team, BBC School Report, Debate Mate, anything that was thrown at me. I guess I wanted something to occupy me. I built fantastic relationships with some of my teachers. To some I can say I owe my life. Mr Wong, my performing arts teacher. Alongside teaching he was a poet, theatre practitioner and playwright. He gave me the confidence I embody today. I could tell him anything. Any situations I found myself in – a girl I had a crush on, an incident in the playground – he would always give me advice. The drama studio where he worked was my safe haven. After school or during break times I would always find myself there.

Mr Melvin, who unfortunately passed away, was a champion for young people. He introduced the BBC School Report and Debate Mate into the school, enabling me to eye a career in the media in the future. Mr Reid never actually taught me. He was the A-level psychology teacher. He had words of wisdom for me always and told me I could achieve whatever I wanted to achieve. It isn't every day that you find teachers like these I've mentioned, who go above and beyond to ensure I had the best future possible.

I did have some bad experiences. There was one teacher in particular who didn't agree with me taking part in all of my extra-curricular activities. Perhaps part of his anger was justified, that I shouldn't have let what I did in my spare time take over my studies. One day in class we ended up having an argument. I had mixed up the dates to hand in an assignment, so I should rightly have been punished. However, he used this as an opportunity to push me two sets down.

I was so discouraged. I felt it was an unfair and unjust punishment. However, this gave me the motivation to focus on this subject. This occurred in my final year at school, I wanted to prove him wrong. Within my classes I made sure I listened to all that was said; I would do extra research and ensure all of my assignments were in on time. And on GCSE results day, I found out that I had achieved an A* for my hard work.

*

Looking back, at the age of twelve or thirteen, I was at a crossroads. Most people assume that you get your education in the classroom, but actually school is only one small part of it. One key aspect of my early life was my local youth club. I used to visit the club regularly in my early years in secondary school. Me and my friends would go and play football and participate in different workshops. My youth club was really cool because a show that was recently introduced on TV had been filmed there. *Meet the Adebanjos* was a comedy show about a normal Nigerian-British family.

Following on from primary school, the youth club was another place where I could pursue my interests, gain encouragement from adults I trusted and, perhaps most importantly, relax and have fun. As well as having access to game consoles and play areas, the club also ran a busy programme of talks, bringing in local businessmen, artists, politicians and sports stars to talk to us about their journeys and give us advice on how to succeed. I can't say that they were all useful. I distinctly remember an accountant who came to talk to us about money management, but ended up lecturing us about mortgages. None of it made sense. We just thought, We're thirteen. We're just about able to buy sweets for ourselves. Why are you talking to us about home ownership? However challenging the talks were, though, they also offered something important — visions of the future. The speakers were saying: we were in your position once and look where we are now. You are more than your environment. It started me thinking about what I really wanted to do and how I could get there.

Not long after I started at secondary school, at the age when I was gaining a bit of independence, my youth club was forced to reduce its programming. Its government funding was cut and no other financial backers could be found. It was devastating for the local community and it had a real impact on me. Beyond the activities and resources it provided, it was a space where I could just be me and sit around with my friends. School finished at 3.30 p.m. every day and, like for a lot of my friends, it wasn't always feasible for me to go home. My mum was out working a lot of the time, I couldn't really bring friends back, and, if I did, there wasn't really much for us to do. All of a sudden we had nowhere to go and nothing to do. It wasn't just our youth club that was closed, others were too, as well as libraries across the borough. The hours between school finishing and dinner time stretched on for ever. I was getting bored.

For the years to follow we found a solution. At least three times a week, me and a handful of friends would visit what we called 'Brikky McDs' — the McDonalds in the heart of Brixton, sipping on strawberry milkshakes. Once our youth centre closed, the lack of interactive and engaging activities quickly became a drag. When you are bored you can find yourself in meaningless movements. I was trying my best to remain occupied, but every so often, to have some fun, my friends and I would retreat to the Brixton McDonalds to chill and bond. It was one of the only venues we could all be together and feel safe. However, these were not short visits: on some days we could find ourselves there for hours upon hours. I had days when I was located in this place from the time school finished until late — 10 or 11 p.m. On some days we would spend the same amount of time in Brikky McDs as we did in school, which is crazy to think about. OK, we could be loud and boisterous. People sometimes construed us as being violent or aggressive, but we weren't. We were not being antisocial, we were just being social.

Brixton was a place to make friends. I made so many friendships for life there. We all had nicknames or what we would call tags. I became known as JE. I would meet up with Ziggy, Tintilla, Ace, Riz and Whiltz every day after school. We all attended schools in different areas, but this didn't stop us from being together. Tin and I called each other cousins, even though we were not blood related. He was super popular and this made me semi-popular too. We did have fun all the times we spent together, but we also experienced things that no kids should have to go through.

For those who didn't find anything to do after school, they often found themselves going down the wrong path. I firmly believe the closing of youth services and centres have directly contributed to gang activity. Since 2010, youth services across England have been cut by 69 per cent. Is it any wonder we recently saw such a sharp spike in youth violence?

I was lucky to find another path. Just after I started at secondary school I began to spend a lot more time on various extra-curricular activities. I signed up to anything I thought was interesting, I always liked to be busy. By year nine, I was involved in a number of entrepreneurial schemes and programmes, regularly attended networking events for young leaders, was an avid member of our school journalism club (sponsored by the BBC), was a key singer in the school choir, attended army cadets (which I loved) and I also played a lot of basketball for my local club. I was becoming more and more confident. Most kids my age got up in the morning, went to school, came home, did a bit of homework, watched a bit of television and went to bed. No bad thing at all. But I was doing a lot more and getting a lot more from it. If I wasn't at Brikky McDs, a class or an event after school – singing Christmas carols for charity events, for example – I was at home, learning how to write PR releases with advice and guidance from some of the best publicists in the business.

More than specific skills and knowledge, these activities helped to broaden my education and my appetite for learning in ways that my school simply couldn't. I was not only learning to do things, but I was learning to believe in myself. I was starting to see a future beyond school — a world where I was a journalist, a broadcaster, a musician, a politician, an economist, an entrepreneur. What's more, I was starting to pursue my own projects, building up my charitable foundation, developing business ideas with my friends and mentors. These were not the idle daydreams of a school boy; these were real and achievable goals. I was taken seriously. My education was suddenly tied to something tangible. Extra-curricular activities were another vital building block of my becoming.

It was obviously a busy time for me, but I was able to balance my schoolwork and my extra-curricular activities, just about. In spite of getting my work done, I used to get a lot of frowns from some of the school staff. Just as the support of teachers in primary school encouraged me to apply myself, the negative comments of one teacher suddenly shifted my priorities, and I lost my appetite for learning for a little while. I didn't realise it back then, but my self-esteem was not particularly robust. All it would take was a little comment to dampen my spirits, especially from a trusted figure, like a teacher. When anyone is on the move to develop, it can be especially difficult when individuals put you down, intentionally or otherwise.

*

Damani

I attended Heathbrook primary school in Wandsworth, then I went to Westminster City boys' secondary school in the Westminster/Victoria area. Looking back, I don't think I handled the transition from primary school to secondary school very well. I didn't understand how serious secondary school was, nor how strict it was going to be. I didn't always listen in class, which resulted in me missing out on things that I really should have been paying attention to. I'm not sure why. I suppose at the time, I couldn't see the point. I had no clue what I wanted to do or what I was learning for. I couldn't see a future for myself.

I think a lot of my friends went through the same issues. That said, nearly all of my friends with older siblings settled in quickly. But it felt like I was going through it by myself. I had no one older to look up to, no one to guide me. I think that played a big part in what happened to me.

You are exposed to a lot of negative things in an inner-city comprehensive. Problems that young people from working-class backgrounds experience in their homes and communities are brought to school. Another difference is that students in private schools are exposed to many more opportunities and you get to experience and learn a lot more things that kids in state schools don't.

Socialising is also different. For example, when my siblings go to hang out with their friends, they're going to someone's house because they live in homes with a lot of space. My siblings have friends who live in places like Kensington, and they can go there and just chill or swim in their garden. If they want, they can sit there and read books or they can do something really creative. It's crazy how different it is to how we'd spend our time. Someone in a state school would probably meet at a friend's house, but because they lived in a small flat on a council estate, you couldn't go inside the house. So we'd chill outside. And when you're chilling outside, you start to mix with different people and it becomes something different. Or you end up being seen as a gang, because you're out on the street. And this is because you are less fortunate than those with big houses or money to do activities; you've got nowhere to go and nothing to do, so all you know is hanging outside or in a park. It's humiliating in a way. People might see you as a threat, but really you've just got nowhere else to go.

We grew up in an age of austerity. When we were in year seven, something like 70 per cent of youth services in Lambeth were cut. It was harder in a way, because we were very aware of what we lost. Before secondary school, there seemed to be so many different youth clubs or centres we could go to. We would travel around and if we were going to go to Brixton, I could go to Max Roach or Tulse Hill adventure playground or I might go to Lollard. My auntie was a youth worker so we used to travel around with her during summer to the different adventure playgrounds, but I remember one summer when I was in year seven or year eight, a lot of them closed down. Only some areas still had them and, because there weren't really any youth clubs, more of us started hanging out on the streets and this is when a lot of the gangs I know were formed. And then when a group disliked another, they would form a rival gang.

You'd always find us in McDonalds or KFC. They became our spots, the places where everyone could meet up. After school, someone would ask, 'Where are you going?' You'd say Brixton and everyone would get off the bus in Brixton. Everyone would be just be chilling and meeting and socialising with other kids. It was fun but when a lot of young people would meet after school, especially in their different uniforms, there were always a few that wanted to be the bad guy and show off in front of the girls. And that's how situations would turn bad or escalate.

In secondary school I found that teachers were quick to pick me up on even the smallest transgression. The little chats that I sometimes had in class with my friends, for example. I'm a bit of a talker so when it came to lesson time, even though I'd be doing work, I was always going to socialise. At that age I was trying to fit in with everyone, so I would start up a little conversation with different people in the hope of building friendships. In primary school this was 'talking' and might earn me a telling-off eventually. In secondary school it was 'persistent level 1 talking' or 'low-level disruption' and would earn me a negative point.

These points were part of a behaviour system called SIMS. If you did well, you were given a point. If you misbehaved, you were deducted a point. One point was deducted for persistent level 1 talking. Seriously disruptive behaviour would lose you three points, the maximum amount you could lose in any given lesson.

If you only lost one or two points in a day, they were scrubbed off overnight. But if you lost three points or more, your parents would be notified and your points were deducted from your total tally. I'm not sure I saw many positive points handed out, to be honest. My school only really focused on the negative. Thirty positive points didn't get you anything. But thirty negative points was isolation. Forty negative points was exclusion. Six exclusions was permanent expulsion. So I was getting a lot of minus points for low-level disruption and I just wasn't learning. I used to talk and talk and talk and, even though I was doing all of my work (and doing it well), every lesson I would just be collecting minus points. Then all of a sudden, I was told I had reached minus thirty points — isolation or internal exclusion. I was sent to a room for a whole day to do my work with other students who were at minus thirty points. We were all in our own separate corners, so we couldn't talk or get up and interact. We had our breaks in there. The teachers brought us in our lunch to eat at our desks. All I did in isolation was write lines. I can't remember the lines exactly, but they were something like: 'I will do my work and I will do what I have to do in class'. I sat and wrote lines all day long.

I felt like I was in prison. I had no agency, no control. I was given food and told to eat it. I didn't speak to anyone all day. There was little else to it. I wasn't told why I was in isolation. No one offered me guidance or admonish-ment or support. Nothing. I didn't realise what it would lead to. I didn't understand the severity of the situation. It all felt so minor and so unfair. So I was back in class the next day, racking up minus points again. And then I hit minus forty. I got home and my mum said she'd had a call from the school telling her that I was excluded for a day. That was it. So I came back in the day after and ended up doing the same thing again. Eventually, I was permanently excluded. I heard a little while later that the school was considering re-admitting pupils who had been expelled as part of the SIMS system, but for me it was too late.

I am not sure I would say that I was expelled, really. It felt more like I was pushed away. I believe that the SIMS system was designed to target the most troubled or struggling students and keep them away from the other pupils. There was a pressure to perform. I am sure that academic results had a lot to do with it. It also felt like once you were identified as someone who wouldn't succeed, that was the end for you. Pupils who had been excluded or sent to isolation were marked and were more likely to get more negative points. Occasionally I would check my profile and see negative points from teachers I didn't even know. It was as if I was blacklisted. I was 'Damani, the disruptive one' and so that's how I was treated, even though I was getting on with my work. The whole thing felt like a set-up. Like I was judged to be unlikely to achieve good grades and so was set up to fail.

In my first year at secondary school, I was excluded five times; four times from the SIMS system and once for a situation that took place outside of school. Honestly speaking, on that occasion, I was with someone who had stolen something from a shop. They found out that I was there through CCTV so, even though I hadn't stolen anything, I was excluded straight away. All the other exclusions were through the SIMS system. In year seven alone I reached 144 negative points from low-level disruption in class. They had it all logged.

I was stupid and immature, I can't lie. Especially in my first year. But I was given no guidance. No one sat me down and tried to encourage me to think differently. I was back in class and, almost as quickly, I was out again. I did start to learn, eventually. In year seven I had 144 points and five exclusions, but in year eight I only received fifteen negative points. So I think naturally, as I was a bit older, I started to understand things a bit more and, in the end, I was expelled for a separate incident, not because I hit the maximum points allowed.

There were a couple of teachers who tried to help me. My form tutor, Mr McManus, for example. I remember him. He always tried to help me out, give me a helping hand, but he had limited time to work with me. I would see him

*for, I think, fifteen minutes in the morning and ten min-
utes in the afternoon. There was also a support teacher in
my class who would always look out for me. These teachers
both tried to help put me on the right path, but I spent very
little time with either of them. If I'd had more time with
them, it's likely my actions would have changed or they
would have been able to give me that intervention that I
needed.*

*Eventually I was permanently excluded. The first thing I
realised was that this was no small thing. I hadn't realised how difficult it would be to get into another school.
On top of the stress of getting kicked out and losing my
friends, I also had very few options in terms of what to do
next. I was fourteen and almost out of options. It was
crazy.*

*The worst part of it was facing up to my parents. I felt
sorry for my friends who weren't getting the support they
needed at home. Even before I got kicked out of school, my
parents were on my case to fix my behaviour and they
were there for me at a time when I needed them the most. I
know there were others whose parents were too busy or
didn't have the time for them, which would definitely have
made the whole experience harder to go through.*

*Mainstream schools weren't an option, and so I was
sent to a Pupil Referral Unit (PRU) fairly near to me. I
think it's important to mention that there are differences*

between the PRUs you can go to. Where you are sent largely depends on the reason why you got kicked out of school. There was a PRU where you'd go straight into doing a trade, so mechanics, electronics or computing. You could be sent to what was just a bad PRU. God help you if you were sent to a bad PRU. There was no hope for the people there. It was basically a day-care centre, not somewhere they would ever receive an education. Then you have ones that try and help you, like the one that I went to, Park Campus (PC). At PC, depending on your behaviour, you could be selected to go into the reintegration programme. This was where they would focus on your behaviour, show you what you should be doing and put you on the right path to go back into a mainstream school. They would also start doing applications for mainstream schools for you to see who'd accept you. If you were lucky, you'd be accepted back, and if not, you stayed there.

I was in the PRU for about two years. Two very critical years, in terms of my education. Not only did PC show me what I shouldn't do, they also showed me what I should be doing in school. They sort of trained me into being the student that I should have been in the first place. After that I went back into education and I finished secondary school in a mainstream school.

The PRU was very different to what I was used to or what I had gotten used to. The uniform at the PRU was just a school jumper. You could wear trainers and black trousers with it. Going back into mainstream education, I had to buy a school blazer, tie and a school bag. At the PRU, our homework would just be a piece of paper, so I never used to carry a bag, I would put things in my pocket. So I had to learn to remember to carry a PE kit, my books, homework, pens and pencils.

I was in the PRU when I had to pick my GCSE subjects. As you can probably guess, your GCSEs shape everything that follows after. A-levels or other college qualifications, university applications, jobs, careers, families and so on, and so on. And at the PRU, the only GCSEs I could take were maths, English, science and one other.

Even if you were doing really well in school, academically, your options would almost always be limited at the PRU. Well, actually, it depends on the PRU. At my PRU, we could only study four possible subjects. But at Park Campus, if, for example, they saw you were good at PE, they would let you join the PE club. I was lucky in that I was interested in subjects they offered as GCSE options – resistant materials and design technology, in my case – but there were plenty of my friends and peers who weren't able to study subjects they wanted to. By the time I got back into mainstream school, there were a lot of subjects that I couldn't pick up because I hadn't been able to study them in the PRU. Subjects like history or religious studies, I didn't know enough about them to take them on as GCSEs.

I was learning, but learning very slowly. What needs to be taken into consideration is that, in a PRU, there are a lot more people with behavioural needs than in a single mainstream classroom. The teachers there are trained to deal with or handle this — so the way for a good PRU to be run is for them to be suitable for and take into consideration these behavioural needs.

My friends who went to PRUs followed different paths. A couple of them were killed, God rest their souls, and quite a few of them are in prison. I think that, because they weren't in mainstream education – and didn't have to be as focused as students in mainstream education – they had a lot more time on their hands to get caught up in stuff that they shouldn't really have been doing. Things like gang activity or selling drugs. Just different stuff. Some people were stealing, robbing people, involved in crazy and dangerous things.

It's easy to see why you would get caught up in the wrong things. At a PRU, you're at the bottom of the barrel. You're always the last to be checked on. You're made to feel like nobody really cares about you and there's no hope for you. And that's not true. There are lots of people who've gone to PRUs that I don't think people would know had gone there. There's a rapper named Frosty who went to the same PRU I did, who is now signed to one of the biggest record labels in London. He had potential and a lot of young people in PRUs have potential for lots of different things, but they're not pushed in that direction; or they're told that they can probably never get there, instead of being told that, despite their circumstances, anything is possible.

As bad as it was that I was left in a PRU for two years, I think Park Campus helped me in the sense that I came into contact with so many different types of people. I ended up there because I was immature and disruptive, but going there helped me to grow up and see the bigger picture. That didn't and still doesn't work for everyone who goes to a PRU, because everyone in there is different and not every PRU cares enough about the young people there. There were kids like me who just liked to talk, but there were also some kids in there who had done quite bad things and, by just dumping them in a PRU, the potential to do any better was written off. If as much effort was made to care about them as they care about school league tables, there wouldn't be so many of them in prison or dead.

I think students, especially those with behavioural needs, should be shown how important it is to stay in school and to study, and be shown the opportunities that come from it. Because although we all go to school and learn, I didn't really understand what learning meant at that age or how far it could get you in life. At the time you're just seeing work and homework, work and homework, but you don't understand that this is all just preparation to help you get to where you want to be in life.

*

The experiences described in this chapter should make two things clear. First, people from underprivileged backgrounds can succeed in our education system, like I did. Second, many are all too often pushed out, and left to find their own way. This is what happened to Damani.

Damani's experience is not rare. Too often teachers do not have the time or resources to adequately meet the needs of disadvantaged children, so they are forgotten. Our education system just isn't equipped to level the playing field for everyone. Like I said before, I strongly believe that one inspiring teacher can transform your life. But I also believe that one bad teacher can destroy your education. I've heard teachers say to my friends that they won't amount to anything, that they are from nothing. It can become a self-fulfilling prophecy.

Weaknesses in our school system will inevitably disadvantage those young people who already have less in life. Young people bring their problems to school. Because of the stresses that poverty can cause, such as those I described in the previous chapter, there will be greater needs to be met in poorer schools. The consequence is that many schools, unless they are given the resources they need, will likely have to focus on discipline instead of finding what makes young people tick. My experience has shown that for young people like me to succeed, there needs to be an array of activities and pathways available for us to go down. The alternative is that young people like Damani don't just get left behind, they get forced out of the system.

Of course, that our education system discriminates is not something you should believe from two stories I have told you, of my own and Damani's. However, broader evidence is also clear that our school system is failing pupils from disadvantaged backgrounds. A recent BBC report concluded that at our current rates of academic progress, it will take fifty years to close the gap between rich and poor pupils. Again, our education system just isn't equipped to level the playing field for everyone.

As I will explain in a moment, there are some promising trends in secondary education, and ideas that should be adopted. However, there are also aspects of education which I think are getting worse. For example, the increasing focus on test results means that the creative subjects that made me who I am will fall by the wayside. This is particularly worrying in a context where the government and many schools don't seem to value the arts. One consequence of this is that between 2010 and 2018 there was a 35 per cent decrease in arts entries at GCSE. None of this is to say that maths and science are not important subjects, but I do wonder what happens to pupils who are less academic and more creative. Creative subjects promote reasoning, innovation and imagination – the things that we actually need more of in the world to solve our problems, I believe.

One thing I think we should never lose sight of is that everyone is different. This goes beyond test results and subject choices, although that is large part of it. As we have seen in this chapter, poverty can be the cause of a number of associated problems in school, from lack of parental support to fatigue and malnourishment. A pupil who is not performing well and is not always behaving properly is at risk of exclusion or expulsion. Again, the statistics here are clear. The government's own data shows that children on free school meals – a key indicator of poverty – are four times more likely to be excluded than the rest of the school population. Pupils of Irish Traveller, Gypsy/Roma and black Caribbean, or mixed white and black Caribbean heritage are also significantly over-represented in PRUs. Schools will justify such statistics by claiming any exclusions are to protect the learning environments of other students, but there are concerns this is done for more cynical reasons. In a recent *Guardian* article the poet and educator Michael Rosen questioned whether exclusions were being made 'solely on the basis of benefiting students and teachers' or if they were being used as 'a way of benefiting a school's position on the local league table?'

We shouldn't underestimate the impact exclusions can have on a young person. This has short-term and long-term aspects. In the short-term, excluded pupils are twice as likely to be taught by an unqualified teacher or a temporary or supply teacher, and a recruitment crisis for leadership staff in these schools means that few excluded young people with have the positive experience I had with the headteacher at Tenisons. This is one of many reasons that less than 2 per cent of excluded pupils get a 'good' pass in English and Maths at GCSEs. In the longer term, we know that 50 per cent of PRU pupils are unemployed and out of education by the age of sixteen and that an enormous 89 per cent of prisoners at Young Offenders Institutions have been excluded at school. Beyond the cost to the individuals involved, the Institute for Public Policy Research (IPPR) calculated the lifetime cost of one year's cohort of officially excluded young people to be nearly £2.1 billion.

Given the information presented above, it seems like it should be a no-brainer for the government and schools to try and reduce the number of people excluded from school. However, all data shows that schools are generally moving in the opposite direction, and between 2013 and 2018, the number of permanent exclusions in

England has increased by 60 per cent. This is particularly shocking if you are from a background like mine, where almost everyone I know who ended up permanently excluded is now dead or behind bars.

However, one school in south London is showing it doesn't have to be like this. And that there is another way. Dunraven is a school in Streatham in south London which runs from nursery age all the way up to year thirteen. It is exceptional because, in a period when nationwide exclusions have rocketed, Dunraven has decreased their permanent exclusions to zero. In addition, they have only had 14 temporary exclusions, which pales in comparison to the national average of 174. Dunraven is an inner-city school in Lambeth, with almost half of their students coming from low socio-economic homes. So what makes them so different to the rest?

Dunraven's headmaster David Boyle made it his mission to reduce permanent exclusions to zero and, instead of punishing children for their behaviour, in 2012 he put in place a system that works alongside and supports young people to reintegrate them back in to class. To do this, he created an on-site inclusion unit, called the Base, where young people at risk of being permanently excluded can still learn whilst working on managing their behaviour. Sixty young people used the Base last year and all were successfully reintegrated back in to the main school. In contrast to a PRU, where many young people are left to their own devices, the Base appears to take the time to understand the reason behind the disruptive behaviour. Some prefer the Base as the main classrooms are too loud, while others are there because of constantly getting into fights. Whatever the reason for being sent there, the Base is changing the way disruptive young people are treated and making sure that, despite the issues they are going through, they are given every opportunity to thrive, just like their peers. It's an approach where they are not just seen as bad kids and punished, but just as kids and given another chance to succeed. I believe the success of this project shows that more interventions where young people aren't criminalised for their behaviour are needed in schools around the UK, and I hope that this is a model that the education system will seriously consider taking on board.

The final aspect of our education system which I want to address is mental health, because I think it is such a core issue which is currently under-explored. In a study conducted by Big Change, half of school leaders said that teachers cannot recognise poor behaviour linked to mental health problems. There is a correlation between exclusion and poor mental health in later life, which makes more sense if you think that a lot of excluded pupils may have been suffering from undiagnosed mental health conditions in school. I cannot begin to imagine the confusion and frustration of suffering from a mental health condition that you cannot make sense of. What is even harder to contemplate is the idea of those pupils most in need of help being punished and ostracised.

We need an education system that can allow people from all backgrounds, and with all different talents and capabilities, to flourish. We need strong mental health education in our system so that young people feel listened to and supported. This means a culture change, like the one implemented in Dunraven. It also means better training for teachers to recognise and be able to act on the issues that are affecting young people from backgrounds like mine. Ultimately, this will all require more resources for teachers and support staff so that young people can benefit from an education that works for them, and empowers them, not one which punishes young people when they are unable to conform.

*

I have a question for you. What is education? I don't mean the education system, but education itself. I decided to leave school at eighteen. The reason that I chose not to go to university (straight away, at least) was because I believed that I could learn a lot more outside of the classroom. And, so far, I think I made the right decision.

There are skills that we simply cannot learn in a traditional educational setting; skills that will actually help us to thrive and solve problems in today's world. We need to shift our outlook on what education is and what it means, and change our language, actions and institutions to reflect that.

For young people reading this, I encourage you to try and answer this question, have conversations like these with your family, and explore what you really want to learn about and why. For family members, don't stigmatise or pressure others into certain choices; instead, support and listen to them to help them to find a path that is best for them and not for anyone else.

In every organisation, in every culture, people thrive because of the people around them. It is important to create an environment in which young people from deprived backgrounds can work together and support each other. Education can't just be left to schools. We need investment in youth and community centres and projects. We need to surround children with positive individuals and messages. We need to better support our teachers and change the image of the profession to encourage the best minds to pursue careers in education. More than anything else, we need to give more children another chance. It will be worth it. Because irrespective of background, gender or socio-economic class, any child can be a success. I am testament to this.

4

Justice

It was a Friday evening in south London. A warm, summer evening, bringing with it the mix of relief and excitement that Friday evenings in early summer in south London always bring. You know what I mean. This Friday I was particularly excited. I was on my way home from Army Cadets, thinking about what to wear to my good friend Denia's eighteenth birthday party. From the amount of planning Denia had done and the number of conversations about it in the past few weeks alone, it was looking set to be one of the best parties of the year. Unfortunately I couldn't go too crazy. I had a first-aid competition with the Army Cadets early the next

morning. The whole of that afternoon we'd been practising CPR, wrapping bandages, carrying stretchers
back and forth. If you've never been an army cadet, you
might be wondering what a first-aid competition is. It's a
series of simulated events in which you are tested not
only on your first-aid skills but also on your response
time. It's a lot of fun, but not the kind of thing you want
to do if you've had a few drinks the night before. I wasn't
entirely sure how I was going to get up in time for the
competition, but I thought that with a couple of alarms
and a little kick of caffeine I would be alright.

I got home and started to get ready: box-fresh limited-
edition Nike trainers, a pair of D&G black slim-fit jeans
and a Disturbing London black tee. My friends knocked
at the door, and together we walked over to Denia's
house, just round the corner. Almost as soon as we got
onto Denia's street, we could tell the party was well
underway. There was music playing, people standing
around talking and laughing, and a big group of girls
disembarking from a taxi just outside Denia's house.

We made our way in and found a spot in the kitchen to
stand and have a drink. The house was completely full.
Some people were chatting in clusters, some were dan-
cing. I tried to talk to my friends, but was distracted by
the sight of one of my childhood crushes in the corner.
I thought I should go over and say hello, but I didn't
know the best way to approach it. Should I bump into

her by accident, start a conversation with a pick-up line, or just play it cool and hope she gave me some attention? I stood there awkwardly, wondering what to do, when my friends nudged me to go outside.

Almost as soon as we got outside, everything changed. I heard the sound of glass shattering. Then I heard screams, followed by shouting. Then, over the noise of the party, the heavy footsteps of people running. A dozen or so young people rushed around the corner and right past us, a look of terror on their faces. I asked what had happened, but no one answered. I didn't know what the hell was going on. Baffled, we walked around the corner. In the middle of the pavement was a group of people, surrounding something or someone. A girl on the edge of the circle was crying hysterically. Another girl broke away and started walking towards us, her face blank. I asked her what had happened; she said that a boy had been bottled, hit in the head. I pushed through the circle and saw him. He was standing in the middle, with what looked like a red cloud spreading out across his T-shirt. Suddenly, he collapsed. No one moved, but my first-aid training kicked in. As I walked towards him, I was stopped by another boy, who shouted, 'Don't go anywhere near.' I tried to explain that I was a first-aider and he let me through.

I knelt down beside the boy and took a look at him. He had a few small cuts on his head, but it didn't look too bad. His T-shirt was completely red by now and a pool of blood was beginning to spill out underneath his body. One of Denia's neighbours was pressing tissues or napkins onto his T-shirt; he told me he'd been stabbed.

'My name is Jeremiah, I'm a first-aider,' was all I said. I'm not sure why. All I could remember was my DR ABC: Danger, Response, Airway, Breathing, Circulation. Were we in any immediate danger? No. Was the casualty responsive? Yes. I didn't need to worry about ABC – checking his airways, checking he was breathing, administering CPR – for now, but he didn't look good. The neighbour pulled up the boy's T-shirt to apply more napkins. I had never seen a stab wound in real life before. It was a long tear in his flesh, but it didn't look that deep. He must have been stabbed elsewhere to be losing so much blood. Me and the neighbour managed to place wads of napkins on all the wounds we could find, as someone spoke to the emergency services on the telephone. People from the party began gathering around, and I begged people to lend me their brand-new jumpers, belts and shirts to help stem the bleeding. I was kneeling by the boy's chest, my head in line with his head. I suddenly remembered that another key priority when administering first aid during a trauma incident is to make sure that the casualty is alert and awake. OK, I thought. I've just got to keep this guy talking.

I remember looking at his face and thinking he was like a weak light bulb, flickering on and off. He was there one second, then gone, then back, then gone, then back. I had to keep him in the present. The first thing that came into my mind was music. I asked, 'What music were you listening to this morning?' And he replied, 'Stormzy. "Shut Up".' I couldn't think of what else to say. 'Um, do you think Stormzy is a cool person?' The boy must have been in shock, because he was trying his best to answer my stupid questions properly. I asked him to recite the lyrics. It wasn't the best moment for a sing-along, but for some reason getting him to repeat the lyrics made a difference. I joined in with him. All that mattered was that he was awake and alert.

Eventually the police arrived, brought out their own first-aid kits and cut off the boy's clothing to assess his wounds. I was still kneeling by his head, talking to him and applying pressure to the wounds that the police officers hadn't got to. I can't lie, in that moment I was praying. Praying that he would be OK. Praying that I had done enough to help. It's a stupid thing to say but, although I had never met the boy before, I couldn't imagine what I would do if he didn't make it. The police kept me where I was, applying pressure, talking non-sense and praying like crazy.

A few minutes later the paramedics arrived. I have never been so happy to see anyone before in my life.

They checked his vital signs, stopped as much of the bleeding as they could and got him onto a stretcher. Without thinking, I picked up his shattered phone and called my own number. I knew that you couldn't just call up hospitals to get an update on a casualty, but I wanted to be able to check if he was OK. As the boy was taken into the ambulance, I handed his phone over and said, 'Don't worry about nothing. God's got you.'

My friends walked me back to Denia's house. Everyone had gone. Denia's mum, who I call Aunty, walked me out to the garden and washed the blood off my hands and arms with hot soapy water. I felt totally fine. Apart from the blood that was now running onto the grass, it was almost as if what had happened had never occurred.

I could hear a loud banging from inside the house and then my mum's voice: 'Jeremiah! Where are you?' After seeing blue lights after blue lights flashing past our house, she had feared the worst. Denia's mum wrapped me up in a towel and my mum walked me home. As soon as got in, I remember feeling completely exhausted. I said goodnight to my mum and climbed into bed with my clothes on. But the second I closed my eyes, something happened. I became panicked, upset and overwhelmed with anger. Even though my eyes were closed, I began to see every little detail; the spreading red cloud, the huge cut, the boy's eyes flickering in and out.

Eventually I sat up and started scrolling through my phone. I texted one of the boys who was there when I was administering first aid, asked if he knew who the victim was, and if he was OK. He texted back, saying that his name was Daryl, but he hadn't heard anything about him yet. I wondered where Daryl was, if he had anyone in hospital with him. I hoped he was OK. Looking at my phone, I remembered that I had called myself from Daryl's phone before he was put in the ambulance. I checked my call log and there it was.

I texted him a simple 'Get well soon' message. I waited for ten minutes or so, staring at my phone. No response. So I sent a follow-up message, explaining who I was and then two more messages after that. Nothing. For the next hour or so I kept checking for a reply. I was going to have to get up and leave for the competition soon. Could I go, not knowing what had happened? What if he was dying? What if he was dead? What if I could have done more to save him?

*

On 23 January 2020, just as I was making the final changes to this chapter, I spotted a copy of the *Evening Standard* with the headline 'LONDON KNIFE CRIME HITS RECORD HIGH'. According to official figures from the Office for National Statistics, there were 15,080 knife offences recorded in London in the previous year. It's not a London problem either. In the same period, levels of knife crime broke records across England and Wales, with a 7 per cent rise and numbers pointing to 120 incidents a day on average. Responding to the report, Barnardo's chief executive Javed Khan stated that it was 'unacceptable that knife crime crisis continues to destroy so many young lives', and said that 'urgent action must be taken to break the spiral of violence'.

It's clear that what happened to Daryl is indicative of a much bigger problem in society. While I do not want to excuse the violence that continues to plague my community, and communities across the country, I do think we need to better understand its causes and effects. Say the words 'knife crime' to a random stranger and they will start talking about young black men from London. Try it and see. To be clear, although many of the problems I am addressing here affect young people from disadvantaged backgrounds across the United Kingdom, the predominant issues here in terms of public perception are of gender and race. Is knife crime a particular problem among a certain section of society? And if so, why?

You've got to remember here that our own prime minister openly described perceiving young black men as being violent or criminal. Writing in the *Guardian* in 2000, he said: 'When I shamble round the park in my running gear late at night, and I come across that bunch of black kids, shrieking in the spooky corner by the disused gents, I would love to pretend that I don't turn a hair.'

Johnson said he might also run if it were a 'gang of white kids', but wasn't sure. 'I cannot rule out that I have suffered from a tiny fit of prejudice I have prejudged this group on the basis of press reports, possibly in right-wing newspapers, about the greater likelihood of being mugged by young black males than by any other group. And if that is racial prejudice, then I am guilty.'

This is only one small example. It is important to recognise that prejudice against young black men is omnipresent in our society. And that it has real, material effects.

Take stop and search for example. I am a young black man, which means that I am nine times more likely to be stopped and searched by the police than my white peers. How I view society, and law and order, are intimately linked with how society sees me, and how it treats me. Commenting on the statistic, MP David Lammy said: 'Stop and search . . . destroys trust between police and the communities they serve. Stop and search is consistently ineffective at reducing violent crime.'

More fundamentally, I believe that there is a disconnect between the law and justice in this country. To explain what I mean, we need to explore some fundamental questions. What do we mean when we talk about justice? Where do our ideas about the law come from? How closely does the reality of police work and the criminal justice system match the ideals we hold in our heads? What space is there for change?

*

The Bill was always one of my favourite TV shows growing up. I tried to catch it on ITV every Tuesday evening without fail. I loved police dramas and films: *Bad Boys, Rush Hour.* I never dreamed of becoming a police officer, but I loved to learn about their jobs, interviewing witnesses, interrogating suspects, piecing a case together clue by clue. Up until the age of eleven, my only interaction with the police was through my TV set, like most young people.

By the time I started secondary school, however, I began to see a very different side to the police. No one in my school liked the authorities. Anyone who wore that uniform was a 'pig' and anyone who spoke to them was a 'rat'. The police weren't there to protect us, my friends said, they were there to arrest us. Growing up, I was repeatedly told that our community was 'over-policed and under-protected'. It did little to change my views. But as I got older and bigger, those views began to change.

One Thursday evening I received the following messages on Facebook:

oi
drop out of the Lambeth Youth Election
if not I'm going to come to your house and
    blast you
my home area
I'm going to get your brother too

I clicked on the sender's profile and saw a photograph of a man wearing a dark grey hoodie and a balaclava. Clicking through the pictures on his account I saw another photo of the man in a balaclava, a photo of a Rambo knife and, lastly, a photo of a handgun. I started to panic. Was this real? Why was I being targeted? Was my life really in danger?

My mother immediately contacted Lambeth Council, who had organised the election, and we were called into a safeguarding meeting. Just from seeing the looks on their faces as we walked in I could tell that they were taking this very seriously. We were told that the messages would have to be forwarded to the police and they also asked me what I wanted to do about the election. Was it safer to drop out? I said I would think about it.

The police eventually got in touch and we were assigned a case officer. My mum was called in to the local station to talk through what had happened. They told her that they would investigate, and, then ... nothing. I was given no advice, no additional protection, no idea of the next steps. You've got to remember that I was eleven at the time. I fully believed that at any moment someone would jump out at me with a gun. I couldn't sleep. Every morning on my way to school, I'd be looking over my shoulder. Any loud noises or shouts made me jump. I was on the brink of arming myself with a weapon, that's how unsafe I felt. If the police weren't going to protect me, then I would have to protect myself. Surely in this case, it would be justified? But as scared as I was, I knew it wasn't worth the risk. There was still a chance, a hope, that it could have been a hoax, a sick joke.

After a week or two, we received a letter in the post from the police, saying that there would be no further action on the case due to insufficient evidence. I weighed up my options and decided to stay in the election regardless, making perseverance my weapon. The entire experience moving forward would change the course of my life for ever.

*

Daryl

I grew up in South London – Croydon to be specific – and had a happy childhood. I have a few brothers and one sister and we all got on well. Home life was busy but happy. We didn't want for anything.

When I was growing up, being a gangster was pretty much the pinnacle of achievement. If you weren't involved in something bad, it felt like you weren't really cool, if that makes sense. This was ten or fifteen years ago. Being bad back then meant something different to today. There was less knife crime when I was growing up. If you got in trouble, you'd get rushed, or beaten up, instead of stabbed. But by the age of fourteen everyone around me was smoking weed. Deep it, we were in year 8, you know what I mean. Age fourteen, smoking weed, forming little gangs and riding out, all that kind of stuff.

It felt in many ways we were living a dream. Criminality was glamourised – in music, on television, in films, in the neighbourhood – but it was also presented as one of the few options available to us. Growing up there was a real lack of positive role models. There was no one to look up to.

I wasn't a bad child. I liked school, but I was always knew the path it was taking me on wasn't for me. It was get your GCSEs, get your A-Levels, go to university, get an office job, do that for forty or fifty years, and retire. It was that, become a footballer, or become a rapper. That was really it. The only way out. Or go on road, and get money and success that way. I wasn't cut out for an office job, and I always knew I wanted to do something active. The other issue was that I was put in a lower set for some classes. For Maths and English, for example, the best grade I could get was a C, which doesn't set you up for academic success. It limited me, mentally. Irrespective of my abilities, I felt like I was being told I wasn't capable of achieving greatness. I was average, I was mediocre.

So if I couldn't even get an office job, what options did I have? I didn't think I was cut out to be a gangster. I was no good at rapping, or singing. So it had to be football then.

By the time I started playing football properly, I was fourteen or fifteen. I started off late, but I knew I had some skills, so I just put my all into it. I started playing for a Sunday league team with one of my friends. I scored a hat-trick in my first match – bang-bang-bang. So I thought let me give it a go. I moved on to play for a more serious local team. We had training twice a week, a match every weekend. Again, I was excelling. Football became my sole focus. I finished my GCSEs, and decided to pursue the football thing properly.

The problem was, that level of football was really competitive. You had hundreds of boys just as good as me competing for the attention of one or two scouts, and even fewer professional slots. It was about talent, but also a bit about who you know.

I couldn't afford to have a one-to-one coach like some of the kids, so ended up going to a lot of bigger football camps where I was getting little to no attention, all of that kind of stuff. I was also a lot older than some of the kids there, who'd been in the system since they were eight or nine.

Eventually I realised it wasn't going to work out. I was getting nowhere. I enrolled into college to sit my A-levels and try and get into university, but it was a struggle. After my football career ended, I experienced what I would now say was a bout of depression. I lost interest in life. I just felt like I had no prospects, no opportunities. I had friends who were a year ahead, getting ready to go to university, playing football professionally, and I felt like I was left behind, just floating.

I remember going to a party around that time. It was like a little drink up, with bare black youths in the apartment. But we were all just having a little talk. Normally we would just be vibesing, but this one was just a talk. A question came up and I brought up my football story and obviously what happened and then other black youths were like 'Yeah, that happened to me as well.' So I said, put your hand up if you actually tried to be a footballer? Every single one of them put their hands up.

*

My election campaign was a success and only a few short weeks after I had received the threatening messages, I won a seat in the UK Youth Parliament. I was suddenly more than just an eleven-year-old schoolboy, I was a youth representative within my community, with responsibilities for working with the police directly. Over the next couple of years, I attended a one-on-one meeting with the Metropolitan Police Commissioner Lord Bernard Hogan-Howe, spoke at Parliamentary select committees and attended panels at Scotland Yard. I helped to host the Youth Justice Convention and interacted with the Youth Justice Board at the Ministry of Justice. I was working with the police at a senior level, speaking to some of the most influential decision-makers in the country. I felt like I had a voice and could actually help young people in my ends, improving the relationship between young people and the police in some way. I also tried to drive change. I was never afraid to speak out and tell the truth. And there was a lot of truth to tell.

However, whilst I might have been a Member of the Youth Parliament (and eventually, the Youth Mayor of Lambeth), I was still a young black man, which meant that I also experienced a very different side to the police. Let me give you an example. One evening, in early November, I was walking through Angell Town Estate with some of my friends. A police van pulled up, and we were told to stand against a wall. I knew what our rights were:

- A uniformed police officer could stop us to ask questions, but we didn't have to answer;
- A uniformed police officer could stop and search us, but only if they had 'reasonable grounds' to suspect that we were carrying illegal drugs, a weapon, stolen property or 'something which could be used to commit a crime';
- A uniformed police officer could also search us if they suspected that serious violence could take place, we were carrying weapons, or we were in a specific location or area.

I knew that we were stuck on the very last point. It was fireworks season, when young people from different estates would let off fireworks and sometimes throw them at each other, and there had been a bit of trouble at Angell Town Estate the previous night. As expected, one of the police officers asked if we had any fireworks on us. I said no and asked if we could leave. The police officer turned me around and starting searching through my pockets. At this point a small crowd of passers-by and local residents had gathered, including a friend of ours, Manny.

As I was being searched, Manny walked towards us, stopping along the way to spit into a drain. One of the police officers, a white man in his early thirties, saw him and shouted out: 'Don't bring that Ebola anywhere near me.'

You've got to remember that this was back in 2014, when Ebola was rapidly spreading across West Africa, and the fear of a pandemic was high. At first my friends and I looked at each other and laughed, not fully realising how offensive the comment actually was. It was one thing to stop and search us, treating us like criminals in front of the community. It was another to racially abuse a bystander, a boy who was walking over to see if he could help.

When I returned home I was full of anger and decided to report my encounter to the IPCC, the Independent Police Complaints Commission. Something as simple as filing a complaint was, however, extraordinarily complicated. It seemed specifically designed to prompt complainants to give up, but every annoying extra step only made me more determined to complete it. A few weeks later I finally received a response. My complaint had been redirected to Brixton police station – the very people I was complaining about. Unsurprisingly, I heard nothing from the station.

It's worth spending a bit of time here looking at the IPCC. I think it is a crucial example of how the relationship between police and the public, especially people in communities like mine, have been let down by poor government decisions and management of institutions.

The idea behind creating the IPCC was a good one. The idea was that when the public have a complaint about another member of the public, they can go to the police to try to sort it out, or to seek justice. However, this doesn't work in when the complaint is about the actions of the police *themselves*. To have confidence that the police would be held to account for abuses of their power, the public need to know there is an independent body they can complain to. There were hopes that the IPPC would play such a role.

However, soon after its foundation in 2004, it became clear the IPCC suffered from serious deficiencies, at least from the perspective of people subject to abuses of power by law enforcement. That's because, whilst its title suggested the organisation would be independent of the police, the IPCC in fact referred nearly all complaints back to the police themselves. It meant the police were essentially investigating themselves.

This problem with the IPCC wasn't just recognised by people like me, who had made a complaint and not felt it was properly dealt with. Even people at the top of the organisation knew something was wrong. In 2009, one of the commissioners at the IPCC, John Crawley, resigned because he believed the organisation just had a 'veneer of independence' but was not properly holding the police to account. In a piece in the *Guardian*, Crawley cited some jaw-dropping statistics. Of the 29,000 complaints lodged within one year, only 100 were investigated by the Commission itself, the rest were passed on to the police. He states that even 'allegations of serious criminal assault [by police officers] are now routinely left for investigation by the police, although just 1 per cent of such complaints are upheld by the police'. If you got beat up by the police and complained, there was no way you could be confident you would get justice.

It's hard to overstate the implications of such failures for the relationship between the police and young black men like me. It means we have no recourse to justice. It also allows the attitudes of problematic officers to go unchallenged. If officers are not held to account, bad behaviour will not only continue, but could be encouraged, travelling through the ranks of the force, and resulting in humiliating and degrading incidents such as those experienced by me and my friends. It means, at an extreme level, that people could die. In 2017 alone, twenty-three people died in police custody, eleven as a result of being restrained. I am not in a position to suggest precisely what happened in those cases, or who precisely is to blame, but we can't ignore that was the highest number in a decade.

In this context, is it surprising to see some communities openly mistrustful and disrespectful of police officers? Is it really so strange to see people actively fighting against the police?

Because of the widespread recognition the IPCC was toothless, the body was replaced in 2018 by a different organisation, the Independent Office for Police Conduct (IOPC). The IOPC has been given some additional powers and responsibilities compared to the IPCC. For example, in the past, even if the IPCC found a police officer to have committed a wrongdoing, they would only be disciplined if the local police force that employed them agreed. The new IOPC can discipline officers directly. There is also supposed be greater independence from local police forces when it comes to investigations and appeals.

Yet the real test for the IOPC isn't just whether it has enough powers, but how it chooses to use them. Here, the case of Rashan Charles is instructive.

Rashan Charles was a twenty-year-old black man, who, on 22 July 2017, died after being chased and restrained by police officers in Dalston. According to police reports, the incident happened after Charles' car was stopped and he fled the vehicle. He was then pursued into a shop where he placed an object in his mouth and, according to the police, resisted arrest. CCTV footage from the shop, which was widely shared on social media, show the officer throw Charles to the ground, hold him by the neck, and try to reach into his mouth. Charles then needed emergency treatment, and was taken by ambulance to the Royal London Hospital, where he tragically died.

The death of Rashan Charles happened just over a month after another young black man, Edson Da Costa, died following police contact. It was followed by widespread protests by people who both deaths as more example of police abusing their power. The dismay was summed up well by a friend of Charles who told the *Independent* 'Rash was unarmed and he was not resisting arrest . . . I just don't understand the whole taking him down to the ground and choking him and handcuffing him'.

This incident is one of the more extreme examples of why the police don't have the confidence of young black men. But in responding to it, could the IOPC show they were tougher than the IPCC? Well Rashan's family don't think so. After an inquest found that the police officer involved had not caused Rashan's death, and should not be held responsible, Rashan's great uncle, himself an ex-officer with The Metropolitan Police, said the investigation by the IOPC had been 'flawed' and the process had been 'a farce'. Of the outcome he said:

'I do not accept the verdict and findings. Nor do my family and many thousands of people who have seen the CCTV footage showing the final minutes before Rashan's death.'

Acting on behalf of Charles' family, Imran Khan QC, stated:

'Regrettably, the IOPC, not unlike its predecessor the IPCC, has not delivered the accountability and justice that this family deserve and the public require in order to have any confidence in the way in which it deals with and investigates complaints against the police.'

If the aim of the IOPC was to win back trust with the communities affected by police violence, something here has clearly gone very wrong.

*

The death of Rashan Charles is an example at the extreme end of relations between our communities and the police. However, it is the sharp end of a much wider problem. I believe all the bad incidents between young black people and the police, whether big or small, are connected.

Small things lead to bigger things. As I described earlier, myself and Manny experienced what could be seen as low-level or casual racism, but it's easy to picture something far worse. In many ways, Manny was lucky. According to police data, a black person is four times more likely to have force used against them by a Met police officer than a white person. What we experienced that day was the same callous disrespect and attitude that leads to incidents of injustice that are much more severe. It's the same attitude that would lead an officer to 'honestly believe' that someone who looked like Mark Duggan would be carrying a handgun and shoot him in the chest.

Finally, I should be clear that respect works both ways; not all officers are bad and not all young people who look and dress a certain way are involved in crime. I have described above the negative, and often tragic, effect that the abuse of power by police officers can have on young people like me but the rise in violence against police officers is also a cause for alarm. The number of assaults on officers on active duty have risen by a third between 2015 and 2019. PC Andrew Harper lost his life on duty in August 2019. I have no interest in attacking the police for doing their jobs, but new channels of communication and a new dialogue are desperately needed.

*

In the summer of 2019, I was invited to a block party on an estate near where I lived. Every year within our communities, young people throw block parties in their areas. They are opportunities for the community to come together to eat, drink, dance and have a good time. For us, block parties were a way to celebrate the summer and spend time with our friends and loved ones. For the authorities, they were disasters waiting to happen.

Not long after I arrived at this particular block party, we heard the sound of sirens. Four or five police cars and a couple of police vans came screaming into the road where the party was being held, blue lights flashing. Thirty police officers ran out to break up what was, at that point, a very peaceful and quiet gathering. There was shouting and arguments on both sides. The police said that the party was a 'disturbance', an unlicensed music event. It had to be stopped. One of the organisers, a man named Clive, asked the police to look around.

Everyone was enjoying themselves, there was no trouble, only 'good vibes'. Did the police really need to be so heavy handed? The police believed they did. They tried to force people to move on but, as much as they pushed, the more the people stayed put. 'Why should we leave?' they shouted. And I agreed. Most of the people at the party decided not to move and continued playing their music. In response, the officers surrounded the entire area, refusing to allow anyone back in once they had left. Things were getting tense very quickly.

In the midst of the stand-off, one police officer had taken charge, directing his colleagues and shouting repeatedly for everyone to 'calm down'. I decided to go over to see if I could defuse the situation in some way. 'Hello,' I said. 'My name's Jeremiah.' I held out my hand. 'Inspector Rowe,' the police officer said. I could tell he was already exhausted. I said that I had been a part of the neighbourhood since I was a kid, and started talking about my community work. I was calm, quiet, respectful. As I spoke, I noticed his attitude towards me change. Inspector Rowe was intrigued. Suddenly I was more than a black boy in a baseball cap. I might be someone to be taken seriously.

I explained that everyone appreciated the police doing their jobs. Without the police London would not be a safe place. But, due to the experiences of some of the young people present, hostility was inevitable. For them, the whole force was corrupt. A gang of bullies, nothing more. I explained that for many of these young people the event was one of the few ways they could relax and enjoy themselves safely. Inspector Rowe nodded along and began to respond. He said the police had a duty to keep the community safe and enforce the law. As we didn't have a permit for the party, it was illegal. He talked about the violence in the area and the number of young people murdered or badly hurt. If being heavy handed meant one person was saved, then he felt he had made the right decision. We didn't agree and it made no real difference to their strategy, but I felt that we were speaking as people, as opposed to police officer and law-breaker. We definitely found a middle ground. I mentioned that I had one request. Please, in your debrief could you let the officers know that young people are not all bad. Expect the best from us and you may get the best. It wouldn't be hard to find a way to work together to run events like this successfully. We shook hands and I walked back to my friends.

*

Daryl

So fast-forward a couple of years and I'm nearly finished university. I went back to school, passed my exams, and got a place at Coventry University, studying sports science. It was good few years. I enjoyed my course, and did well. Before I finished, I got chatting to a friend from school who had similar dreams to me, and had lost out on a football career just like me, and we decided to set up a training company together.

I had just bought my very first car, a Vauxhall Astra 2005. I had passed my test the year before, but it had taken me twelve months to save up £1,300 – just about enough. The car was actually £1,350, but the seller let me off the £50. I didn't have enough money for insurance however, so it sat outside my house for a while.

The day I finally got to drive it was the day of a good friend's birthday party. I spent the morning cruising around, a bit overexcited, and finally pulled up the party at about 8 or 9. It was already going off. You could hear the music from around the corner. A girl I knew came over and sat in the car with me – I was chirpsing, you know, feeling like I was the guy because I was in my new car.

A group of boys were walking down the road towards us, and as they got near, one of them walked around to my side and tapped on the glass. He said, 'Where you from?' Now, there is no good way to answer that question. If I said local and they were from outside the area, I was in trouble. If I said outside the area and they were local, I was in trouble. I thought I should just be honest. 'I live around the corner. Why?'

All of a sudden the windshield smashed – one of the boys had hit it with something. I couldn't believe it. My new car! I went to get out and shout at them, but as I opened the door, the boy who'd knocked on the window kicked it closed, so I fell on the floor. Suddenly I was surrounded. One or two of the boys had knives, and I could feel myself getting stabbed and hit – in my head, in my chest, in my legs. I fully realised what was going on, but I couldn't believe it. Never *in a million years did I think that this would happen to me. Eventually they stopped. I was curled up on the ground. They stepped over me and started going through the car, taking my car keys, taking some change I had in the door pocket. Then they ran off. I managed to get to my feet in a daze. A small crowd from the party had gathered and someone said that my head was bleeding. I touched my hand to my head and could see blood on my fingers. I suddenly felt very tired, like my energy was fading. Someone helped me onto the floor, and I started praying, 'Please God, don't let me die.' I didn't want to be one of those kids on the news.*

The next thing I remember is Jeremiah, walking towards me. He had his hood up, and looked like one of the boys who had attacked me. I was terrified. I kind of told him to get away from me, but he came and sat down beside me and started looking at my head and my body. He knew what to do. People had started holding napkins and tissues to try and slow the bleeding, but he told them to stop. He shouted out for towels and clothes and belts, and cut my clothes so he could get at my wounds. He kept talking to me, too, keeping me awake.

After what seemed like forever, the ambulance arrived, and I was taken to hospital. My mum and dad met me there. That was the worst part, I think. Seeing the look on their faces. In hospital they were able to stabilise me and gave me some drugs for the pain. Even then, I was still in more pain than I've ever been in my life. The doctors spent a long time examining me, and told me I was lucky. The stab wounds in my back and chest weren't too deep, and the wounds in my legs had missed my major arteries. I just needed stitches, and lots of rest. But when I was eventually discharged, I couldn't move my back. I thought I had done something to it, that one of the wounds had cut a nerve or something, but the doctors said it was in my head. I couldn't make sense of what had happened. I was the lowest I have ever been in my life. I felt like I had been reduced to nothing. My head had been shaved, my face was swollen, I was covered in enormous bandages. Walking anywhere was painful. My car was a wreck. I had a job interview the next week, which I would have to miss. And all for what?

On the way home, I managed to look at my phone. I had lots of messages from an unknown number, Jeremiah. I wrote back and said I was OK. I thanked him. I really believe I would have died if he hadn't been there. We kept in touch, and he invited me along to a barbecue he was going to. I met him outside the venue, and it was the first time I'd seen him since the attack. I remember just giving him a big hug, and saying thank you. The barbecue itself was unbelievable. I thought it would just be a small south London kind of thing, in someone's back garden. No. This was an event for one of the companies he works with. There was more food and drink than I could ever imagine, lots of famous people. I kind of sat with him in a corner and talked, and he introduced me to everyone he knew. It was unusual to see someone from our background doing the kind of things he was doing, and I found it inspiring. For him, anything was possible. I made a decision to not let the attack impact my life any more than it had.

It took me three or four months to get back to normal, physically. Mentally, I think I'm still recovering.

*

When I was growing up, prison was not a place that I ever believed I'd be visiting. Especially not to see a friend. As I got older, however, it became more and more of a regular occurrence. The first lesson that I learned about prison visits was that you needed to be wearing the correct clothing. There is a 'no hats, no hoods' policy. Typical. You have to take along some form of official identification. You can take in cash, but no more than £20, which has to be converted into change. Be prepared for a long wait as you move through the airport-style security, checking visitors for any contraband, such as drugs or weapons.

I remember my first ever prison visit. HMP Thameside. I remember the weird red building near the entrance. I remember the gates and the barbed wire. I remember walking into the visiting room and seeing him. James. The same James that I'd spent most of the last few years with. The same James I walked to college with, cracking jokes. The same James I would sit in class and complete assignments with, talking about our futures. Then, just before our A-levels, he was arrested. I had only managed to secure a visit about a year into his sentence, as he had been moved around a few times. And here we were, me and James in HMP Thameside. Two young men who used to sit side by side in class were now sitting on opposite sides of a prison table.

In our A-level year, James got into a bit of trouble with a few boys from the local area. It started off as nothing really – a screw-face, a few harsh words spoken – but it escalated quickly. James was attacked and there were threats of more to come. These were boys who were often hanging around our school and in the local area. We ran into them a lot. If there was a group of us together, everything was calm. If James was on his own, he was in trouble. I don't know why they picked on him more than anyone else. It really could have been any of us. One evening I got a call. It was from another friend. 'Have you heard what happened to James?' That evening, James had been on his own when he had bumped into one of the boys who had been giving him trouble. They had a fight and James pulled out a knife. I had no idea he was carrying and I do not condone it, but it made sense. If you knew you could be rushed at any point, what would you do? James chased the boy into a house and tried to get inside. I don't think he would have stabbed him. He was just caught up in the moment.

The police were called and James were arrested. Despite the fact that he had no prior convictions, he received a custodial sentence. And that was that. Fifteen minutes of madness, and his life was changed for ever.

During that first visit we spoke about prison life, and we spoke again about the future. James had no idea what would become of him. In fact, he was fading away. He spent the majority of his day in his cell, with nothing to do and no one to speak to. He was not learning. He was not being challenged. Rather than seeking opportunities, he was attracting trouble.

Prisons, when the system functions as it should, are a way to separate those who abide by the law from those who don't. If you commit a crime, or, at least, if you commit a serious one, then you are removed from society. On those grounds, James's sentence might seem right. He did something stupid, and, for a period, he was separated from society. However, the goal of prison can't just be separation, but also rehabilitation. This is for practical reasons, but also ethical ones. On a practical level, we have to let prisoners back into society, and everyone is better off if, when they return, they are not inclined to commit further crimes. On an ethical level, we as a society have a responsibility not to give up on people. If someone has made a mistake they might need to be punished, but they also deserve a second chance. From everything I know about James' case, prison was is no way set up to give James that second chance. He did nothing there that prepared him for the outside world. It seemed like purely punishment for punishment's sake.

This is of particular concern because if prison doesn't give people a second chance, we are condemning a particular class of people to lives on the sidelines of society. It is not a cross-section of society that find themselves in prison, but disproportionately people from underprivileged backgrounds. A compelling example of this is that, according to a 2016 report from the Prison Reform Trust, half of all children in youth custody in had spent part of their childhood in care, despite only making up 1 per cent of the population in England and 2 per cent in Wales. We can see that people who commit crimes have often been dealt a rough hand in society, they have been excluded somehow. Is prison just compounding that exclusion?

In general, I think the focus of prison needs to dramatically change. At the moment, prisons are not safe, and the government's own statistics show assaults and self-harm in prison to be at an all-time high. This means we are often sending people from one unsafe environment straight into another. How can we expect people to change and grow if they are living in fear? We also need to make sure people leave prison with greater opportunities to flourish in life. According to recent figures,

48 per cent of adults released from prison re-offend within 12 months. That is the clearest sign of a system that doesn't work.

So, we need to reform how prisons work. But we also need to look deeper at how young people end up there in the first place, and make interventions earlier. I spoke in chapter 3 about how the closure of youth services increased the influence of gangs in my area, as young people had nothing to do. That costs lives, as people get stabbed, it also ruins the lives of people who wind up in jail. I would say to the government, and to the tax payers, it is also a false economy. In 2019, it cost, on average, approximately £40,000 to keep an inmate in prison in England and Wales. Cutting money on youth services ruins lives, in the long run it might also cost the government more.

When I look at political leaders in Westminster, I often think they are too far removed from these issues, and so they get overlooked. For that reason, I am particularly inspired by people from the community who, having experienced the sharp of Britain's criminal justice system are working to change it. A brilliant example here is Kenny Imafidon. Like me, Kenny Imafidon is from a Nigerian background, grew up in South London, and was brought up by a single mum. He was an excellent student, got 12 GCSEs and dreamed of being an MP. However, two days after his eigthteenth birthday Kenny was arrested, and charged with murder. The charge was part of a joint enterprise case, which is controversial as it means you can be found guilty by association. Imifado was acquitted of the charge. He was innocent. However, the ordeal meant he spent six months in Feltham Prison. Once released, Kenny spent time campaigning for criminal justice reforms. This included writing reports – called The Kenny Reports, on the issues affecting young people in the UK, in particular the relationship between politics, economics and gangs. He has now presented these reports to at least two Prime Ministers! One of the statistics that stood out to me from his report was that the average murder investigation and prosecution in our communities costs £1 million, and that between 2005 and 2012 he estimated £12 million was spent investigating murders in Lambeth. Those figures make cuts to youth services seem misguided, whoever you are.

I believe that for too long we have had a penal system that focuses on containing rather than preventing crime and providing short-term solutions that are not only costly, but ineffective. The system wholly fails to equip prisoners for the outside world, leading to high reoffending rates.

No progress will be made until factors such as those which contributed to James' imprisonment are properly addressed. He is also an example of why society can't give up on people in prison. Like many others I know, James is a man of many talents, one of them being music. During our conversations, I encouraged him to write, to record his thoughts. So he began to write, and specifically, he began to write lyrics. He spent his time working on a craft which didn't require many resources. Our visits soon consisted of him performing some of the lyrics he had written. When he eventually left HMP Thameside he had already written twenty songs. I helped him release a song that went on to achieve 500,000 streams. James now has a career in music, but he was one of the lucky ones.

*

James made a stupid decision. He takes personal responsibility for that, and he was punished. But decisions also happen in a context, and the decisions young people make are particularly influenced by the society.

We should worry then that in England decisions like the one James made are being landed upon more and more often. In much of this chapter I have talked about the costs of knife crime. We should also look at the solutions.

To work out what it would take to tackle the scourge of knife crime, we can look to an example within the UK:

Scotland, and more specifically, Glasgow. That's because violent crime used to be a huge problem in Scotland, and Glasgow was seen as the murder capital of Britain. In 2004/5 there were 137 homicides in that country. In Glasgow alone there were 40, twice the UK average. By 2018/19 the number in Scotland had more than halved to 60, and in Glasgow that year, only 13 people were murdered.

So what have Scotland got right that England hasn't? Why have murders plummeted in Scotland, whilst in England knife-related homicides are at their highest level since 1947? As Akala brilliantly sets out in his book *Natives*, it has a lot to do with how they *view* violent crime. Since 2005, a decision was made not to view violence as the product of a criminal underclass, but as a public health issue. That crime became not just a matter for the police, but for the NHS, for teachers and for social workers, who's actions would be coordinated in a newly-created 'Violence Reduction Unit', or VRU.

The VRU acted on the principle that 'violence is preventable, not inevitable'. They wanted to stop violent crime *before* it happened. As one part of this, the VRU identified gang members, and invited them to voluntarily attend as session at court. There, they would be told that violent crime in Glasgow would be properly punished, but the interventions were much broader than that. Mothers of people who had been killed with knives would explain to people the consequences of gang violence. The VRU would also offer attendees help with housing, relocation, employment and training, and give them a phone number to call up if they wanted to take up the offer.

A second element of Scotland's approach to violence was that they dramatically reduced the number of people that schools excluded. In 2005 there were 264 young people in Scotland permanently excluded from school, by 2017 that was down to a single pupil. As a comparison, in that same year, 7,720 students were permanently excluded in England.

The success of this approach was phenomenal, with murders in Glasgow reduced by two-thirds between 2004 and 2018. The difference is even more stark if we just look at young people. Between 2006 and 2011, fifteen children and teenagers were killed with knives in Glasgow; between April 2011 and April 2016, none were.

The 'Glasgow Model', as it has come to be known, is therefore something that English authorities should look to adopt. However, I do find it quite odd it was ever considered revolutionary. How could authorities not realise that unless you provide people an alternative to life in gangs, violence will result? How can a government not see that if you exclude people from schools, reject them from the mainstream, they will often end up doing bad things, and making bad decisions? What's worse, in England these lessons still have not been learnt. Like I explained in chapter 3, school exclusions have increased dramatically in recent years, whilst budgets for youth services have plummeted.

*

Daryl

Justice is a big word. I don't feel hate for the people who attacked me, and I can understand why it happened. You've got to break it down and think, where does it really stem from? I think that a lot of the time, it's passed down. This person has stabbed this person and this person has killed my best friend and so on and so on. It's a cycle of retaliation. Once you get in, it's kill or be killed. Or go to prison. There's no other way out. Even if you decided to turn your life around, start going to church, get a job, there will always be people after you. There will always be areas you can't go to. Your best chance is to move out of London completely, start again. But with what? And what are you going to do? Who really wants to hire someone who's got no real skills or qualifications? Will someone who is used to money and a certain kind of life be happy working behind a counter, being bossed around?

It's all too easy to pay attention to the headlines as opposed to the people involved. These young boys were like me. They are angry, and frustrated, and misunderstood, and I feel like they lack a lot of knowledge in the sense of what they can do.

I can't say that youth violence can be eradicated, because it can't be. But, I think that the culture of knife crime, the culture of kill or be killed, the culture of hopelessness, can be disrupted. These government agencies, police, they're not focusing on disrupting the culture, they see it as this is violence and we need to reduce it and eradicate it. Early intervention will help. Youth services and support will help. Mentorship and training in schools will help. Opening up horizons for young people will help. You're always going to have someone who picks up a knife and stabs someone regardless, but the cause is not violence, and it can't necessarily be remedied by the criminal justice system.

Black-on-black violence is a crazy term. Race doesn't come into when there is knife crime anywhere else in the country, or if the victim or perpetrator is white. It just doesn't. Some cities in the UK have a higher murder rate than London. And some have taken a different approach to youth violence. What effect do prison sentences and increased police activity have? In my experience, relatively little. Coming into young people's lives as early as possible and diverting them away from crime, towards the help they need, and towards education and opportunities, that's a more likely solution.

*

In this chapter I have spoken about my experience of the criminal justice system, and the statistics which show how it effects young black men like me. I want to finish by briefly addressing how we *talk* about criminal justice. We need to talk about terminology.

Black-on-black violence. You've heard the phrase a million times. When you open up a newspaper and read about the death of a young person due to serious violence, it is often accompanied by that very phrase. And it's not just the media. In fact, whole police units have been set up to address this supposedly unique 'issue'. Trident and Area Crime Command, formerly known as Operation Trident, is a police division set up in 1998 as a direct response to tackle gun crime and homicide in Lambeth and Brent within the African/Caribbean community. I believe 'knife crime', whilst less explicit, has also come to have a meaning in public discourse similar to 'black-on-black' violence. It might be a neutral term, but when it used by politicians and the media, young black men like me know what they mean.

I remember reading about Operation Trident in several articles and wondering why the black community, which in a 2018 report made up a total of 3.3 per cent of the population in the UK and was the fourth largest ethnicity at 13.3 per cent in London, needed its own police department. Yes, violent crime being committed is serious and by all means needs policing, but when you look at the figures of homicides and violent crimes across the country, the black community weren't leading the pack. This was, as would be expected, mainly committed by white people, who constitute the greatest percentage of the UK population. Yet, when you read about violent crimes where both the victims and perpetrators were predominately white, it is never referred to as being 'white-on-white' violence. Again, as Akala explores in *Natives* (you really have to read that book), there is no department to tackle the disproportionate amount of white on white violence.

We can look further into the facts. Government statistics show that, in the period of 2015/16 to 2017/18, out of 2002 homicides, 246 victims were black and 1,495 were white. In this same period the number of homicides by a sharp instrument saw 456 white victims and 159 black. Whilst the percentage of the homicides by sharp instrument to homicides by race is higher, it is clear that this isn't just a black-on-black problem; it's simply a problem. So why is race then treated as being so important when it comes to serious violence regarding young black African/Caribbean/British men? I believe isolating black men in this way is problematic for a number of reasons.

Let's first look at it this way. Is it true that the entire black community is at equal risk of serious violence? Clearly not. In fact, the factors that lead to more crime are the same across the entire population. Exclusions, whether you are black or white, will make you more likely to commit crime. Poverty too. But by labelling any crime committed by black men as 'black-on-black', we are overlooking all of these factors to say it is just about race.

This segregates young people, and it creates a barrier between black people and everyone else. This generates stigmatisation, and means black people are treated differently. By labelling the crime as 'ours', it becomes something that we exclusively own. The evidence for this is overwhelming. Let's go back to stop and search. Another recent study by the London School of Economics found that black Britons are stopped and searched at 8.4 times the rate of whites, a figure which has doubled since 1998-99 when the MacPherson Report into the death of Stephen Lawrence judged the police to be 'institutionally racist'. There can also be no argument that this is proportionate. The same report found that black people are nine times more likely to be stopped for drug offences than white people, even though black people use drugs at a lower rate than their white peers.

The other issue with the phrase 'black-on-black' crime is that it lets society off the hook. If crime can be dismissed a problem that black people own, it is easier for the rest of the population to dismiss it. It means our country's terrible record on exclusions, on social care and youth work, and on rehabilitations can all be blamed on something called 'black culture'. It's why when I walk past an elderly white lady, she's likely to clutch her bag close, as though my colour means she should be afraid of me by default. It's why the government keep getting away with overseeing rampant injustice and inequality.

5

Business

Early one Saturday morning I found myself in a diner on the Loughborough estate in Brixton, waiting to meet one of my earliest mentors, Karl Lokko. Karl had been once one of the most feared gangsters in London, if not the UK, but turned his life around to become a highly influential community activist, public speaker and advocate for social change. We were meeting that day to discuss a business idea. We were, separately, doing an increasing amount of consultancy work for big companies in the UK, and wanted to find a way to put young, talented people in touch with corporations seeking fresh ideas and inspiration. As well as benefitting the companies we were working with, we wondered if the project could be a way to help those who might still be living the wrong sort of life. I asked Karl a simple question: how many of your former gang members are still in the game?

Karl's answer surprised me. Most, he said, were in prison. Some had been killed. But many were still active. Karl was an anomaly, in choosing a different path. We discussed why this might be. For the majority of people who grow up in the sort of environment that we did, the number of positive role models, especially in terms of possible career paths, are few and far between. For me, at least, it was only my exposure to worlds outside of my own that opened my eyes to what I could become. Anyone from my area, who didn't have the kind of access (through luck, privilege or hard work) that I had, would have a very different vision for their future. A limited one.

I have already talked about how someone's background might influence their future, both in terms of educational attainment, and involvement in the criminal justice system. But I think the relationship between people's class background and our career paths is just as important. The government's own commission on social mobility found that in 2018–19, people from better-off backgrounds were 80 per cent more likely to end up in professional jobs than people from working-class backgrounds. The report concludes that: 'Being born privileged in Britain means that you are likely to remain privileged. Being born disadvantaged however, means that you may have to overcome a series of barriers to ensure that you . . . are not stuck in the same trap.'

This chapter tells a story of what those barriers can look and feel like. It is a story which is partly about attitudes, role models and self-belief. To a large extent, what we can achieve is dependent on what we believe we can become, and that depends on the people around us, and how the rest of society looks at us. It is also about material barriers that face people from working-class backgrounds trying to make it in the world.

In a really simple way, I think about this in terms of my rides on the 345 bus. My end point was very different from my start. Boys of my age in some of the grand houses in Kensington and Chelsea were likely following different models. You follow what you know.

For me, it was the drug dealers or fraud boys with the nice chains, brand-new trainers and expensive cars. People who looked like me and lived in my neighbourhood. People who may not directly encourage other young people to follow their lifestyle, but who provided an example. A simple way to dig yourself out of poverty.

The material reality of inequality of opportunity can also be looked at from the view of the 345 bus window. At the start of a journey on that bus, you see people struggling. Yes, some people have time to think up business plans, or to get qualified for professional jobs. But there are also many people working hour after hour just to feed their kids. If you're struggling to pay your bills, you don't have capital to risk on starting some firm! At the end of that journey the feeling is different. You can almost smell the money and opportunity. Kids my age would be getting private tuition, their path to uni easy, and when they grew up they'd have access to capital to be able to invest, and to take risks.

This is the problem and challenge Karl and I wanted to address. How could we encourage young people who don't have positive role models to believe in themselves? How could we provide the opportunities for them to act on those beliefs? If we could answer both questions, we were convinced we could help create a new generation of entrepreneurs.

One final thing. Before we continue, I want to challenge our understanding of the word 'business'. For me, we need to move away from companies and commercial activity, that all-too-familiar picture of men in suits (white men, all too often), and towards something different. What I understood by business growing up was entrepreneurial spirit. The motivation and imagination you need to transform an idea into reality and to create something for yourself. It's about money, undoubtedly, but it's also about self-confidence, empowerment, initiative and experimentation. It's something I believe we need to nurture more in young people, especially at this current moment in time, if we want to see a new generation surpass the achievements of an old one – a goal that seems increasingly unlikely in this world. As Karl put it that morning, what does success look like? How do we get there?

*

Karl

I am a community champion. I am interested in the local as well as the global. I believe you need to think about both in order to effect real change. I am a pastor and have been involved with the church for almost nine years now. I do a lot of consultancy work and connect with a number of charities. I'm a poet and a writer. I'm also a husband and a father.

When I was fourteen, I was a glorious mess. I'd been cut in the face, stabbed in the chest. At fifteen I lost one of my closest friends. He was murdered by my side. I was very involved with gangs. We made the front page of almost every national newspaper. I had abandoned my education, which is a shame, because I'd always loved to learn. I had taken my year nine SATs when I was in year six, and did well. But by fifteen, GCSE time, I had to make a choice. I couldn't hide it any more. I was derailed, I chose the street. And in that world, I was excelling. I was on my way to achieving my goals. I was a prominent figure in the London gang world. I was also making a lot of music. This was back in the MySpace, Bluetooth era. Back when music used to get passed from phone to phone, playground to playground. I used to calculate my success based on how long it took my music to reach family friends in Luton. How long it took them to get in touch with me about my new music. Sometimes it was only a week. I was a hood celebrity, but I was a mess. A glorious mess.

It was a nightmare, but at the time, it was a dream. I was succeeding. I had street ambitions, back from the age of ten or twelve. From the first time I witnessed a real act of violence. Someone was shot, right next to where we were playing football. And instead of running away, the shooter came over, took off his jumper, and started playing football with us until the police came and took him away. It was traumatic, but it was also romantic. My whole life changed in an instant. I had never seen guns before. I had never really seen violence before. I was traumatised. But there was also something alluring about it. You've got to remember that we had nothing. People from our socio-economic background, *from our areas, were powerless. I felt that powerlessness even at that age: nine, ten, eleven. And the brutality helped to overcome that. All of a sudden I saw someone who looked like me wielding real power. That was how I interpreted that act. It became my dream to follow in that shooter's footsteps. To have the kind of power he had. It was a con, of course. But it was a dream nevertheless.*

Fast forward a few years, and I was at my peak. I had got to the point where I didn't have to do the work. I was like a general, a boss, a CEO. I could just say a word and something would happen. I thought I had arrived. And I had no intention of slowing down. Considering the cards I had been dealt, I thought I had the best possible hand. We were driving German cars, wearing Italian clothes, money in the bank. Meanwhile my parents were still working sixteen-hour days, still unable to make ends meet. I was firmly on my side of things.

I was nineteen and I had it all. Until I suddenly didn't. Until I realised it was all a lie. It was a deception. I was shown that my enemy was not my enemy. The boy across the road who looked like me, but was just with a different group of boys, was not my enemy. Same pain, same struggles, same ideology. Different ends.

In school and at home I had been taught that if I worked hard, I would succeed. I had been taught the difference between right and wrong. Those seeds had been sown, but they had remained as seeds until that point. It was Pastor Mimi who started to water those seeds.

*

Lesson One: Hustle

I started my first ever business at the age of eleven. On my way into my very first day of secondary school, I bought an eight-pack of double chocolate-chip muffins for £1, with the idea of selling them at the bargain price of 50p each at break time. If I sold them all, it would give me a tidy profit of £3. At lunchtime, after meeting some of my new classmates, I asked them if they were interested in my product. I managed to sell two muffins and ended up eating the remaining six. The first business lesson I learned was an important one: never eat your own product.

Even though I had only broken even, my entrepreneurial interests took root. From the simple (and perhaps obvious) muffin business model, I was inspired to think up new ways to make money. The only problem was, when it came to selling snacks, I was a rookie compared to the older kids. Some students were turning over up to £200 a week simply reselling cakes, biscuits and the odd fizzy drink. And if you were just a young apprentice like I was, on occasion you would find yourself getting 'taxed' by the sellers. After handing over a product, an iced-ring doughnut for example, they would say, 'Break me some,' and tear off a piece of the doughnut for themselves. You couldn't really say no if someone asked you to 'break me some'. I was angry, but in awe. That was how to do it. *Sell it* first and then eat it.

Rather than jump back in, I started to watch these business operations within the playground and began to learn a few important lessons. The main thing I realised is that this wasn't fun. Many of my peers were selling as a matter of survival. I knew of one young person in my year group who was a young carer for his mother, but with the added responsibility of looking after his younger siblings. They had next to no disposable income and sometimes not enough food in the house. Selling snacks in school was an opportunity to provide for his family. There were rumours of another boy who was selling snacks to help his older brother pay off a drug debt. We were only teenagers, not anywhere near adulthood, yet making money for some was a must; not for extra pocket money or clout, but just to get by.

Any business will face hurdles and barriers in its early days and selling snacks in the playground is no exception. The biggest barrier at our school came in the form of Mr Thomas, 'the Regulator', the man who would one day bust our operation (yes, I am still bitter about it). Mr Thomas was one of the most feared and respected teachers in the school, and somehow head of year for three separate year groups. During breaks and lunchtime he would stand and watch over us in the playground and even had a network of 'undercovers' (student informants) who would notify him of anyone 'shotting'.

At the time I never understood the school's policy, nor Mr Thomas's mission to stop people making money. Aside from the obvious health and safety risks (people sometimes sold out-of-date products; you had to be careful), it seemed to me to be the easiest way to teach young people about business. We learned the basic principles of supply and demand (no one wanted muffins; I had lots); captive markets (the school cafeteria was awful and no one could escape to buy snacks for themselves); marketing strategies (you were in luck if your name started with the same letter as the snack you were selling); and monopolies (the short period when the school bully got in on the action and scared everyone else off). It felt to me that the snack shop model offered us lessons the school was not providing, lessons that might serve us well in later life. It was a way for young people to provide for themselves. I was proud of breaking even, but some of my peers were dreaming of mega-riches.

Don't believe me? There are two snack-shop legends who will help me make my case. Nathan John-Baptiste, aka 'the Wolf of Walthamstow', was turning over around £25,000 from selling snacks from a school toilet before he was caught. He managed to achieve this extraordinary number by employing an army of students to work for him on a commission basis. Rather than supporting him and helping to develop his obvious talent, he was given several warnings by the school before being excluded.

Or there's Bejay Mulenga. Bejay built on the resale snack shop model, but offered students something different—an accepted tool kit and model they could use to create their own businesses in schools. At the age of fourteen he launched Supa Tuck and within three years had a network of franchises across 100 schools, reaching some 5,000 pupils. Within his first year of trading, he had already turned over an extraordinary £250,000. Also extraordinary was the fact that Bejay operated his sweet shop empire with the full co-operation and support of the schools involved.

These might seem like small examples, but they clearly show that there is space and opportunity for students to succeed if they are given the right guidance and support. But what if they are not? What else can young people do to get ahead?

*

Lesson Two: Nothing to Lose

Following my failed snack initiatives, I continued to experiment. I set up a car cleaning business for a short while, washing cars every Saturday for £15 a go. A little while later, another business opportunity appeared; a family friend asked if I would like to decorate an office building block he had recently rented. A little over-excited, I said yes, not realising that the building was three storeys tall and had dozens of rooms. Two months in and close to despair, I had to think of a new strategy. I began to invite my friends to come along and help, in return for pizza and snacks at the end of the day. We got there in the end but, needless to say, I was very glad when it was over.

To tell you the truth, despite my enthusiasm I was completely lost when it came to the world of business. I had no practical business skills. I knew nothing about money management. I didn't know how to value my time or what I might be good at. I'd developed some soft skills in organisation and marketing from my extra-curricular work, but I didn't know how to apply them or what to apply them to. The closest I'd ever come to building a business model was studying maths, but I couldn't see how Pythagoras's theorem was going to help me kick-start an empire.

And then I saw someone on television who changed my world completely. Jamal Edwards was a young entrepreneur and the founder of the successful music and media platform SBTV, which had helped launch the careers of artists such as Jessie J, Ed Sheeran and Tinchy Stryder. He was speaking about the importance of 'self-belief' and how that had helped him to build his business. A seed was sown. A year or so later, I had the opportunity to interview Jamal on television as part of our school's Young Reporter project, run in partnership with the BBC. To say I was inspired is a bit of an under-statement. At that time, if I could have selected any one person to be when I grew up, Jamal Edwards was it. He was articulate, he was funny and, most importantly, he was encouraging. He talked to me about self-belief and told me that if I ever had a good idea, I should pursue it. Don't pay attention to the voice of doubt or to anyone who's trying to put you down, he said. If you believe in it, you can make it happen.

Not long afterwards I had an opportunity to test this theory out. Through our school project, I had visited the BBC a few times. The BBC at the time controlled the two biggest youth radio stations in the UK: BBC Radio 1, and Radio 1Xtra. However, the BBC itself felt anything but young. The senior staff members I spoke to didn't even seem interested in youth culture. I listened to a lot of radio and followed both stations obsessively, and picked up on a few things that they could perhaps improve on. I was only fifteen at the time, you have to remember, and would be the first to admit I had no real idea about radio programming. I did like music, however, and I thought I knew young people. I was a young person, after all.

I had an idea: the Radio 1 and 1Xtra Youth Council. I wanted to bring together a group of young people from across the UK who could act as an advisory board to the BBC, providing direction on everything from show content to social media strategy, to marketing and advertising campaigns, to corporate social responsibility. It was a good idea, I thought, and so I decided to pursue it. First I had to find someone to talk to.

Ben Cooper was the controller of Radio 1 at the time, and a Very Big Deal, so he was obviously first on my list. After many drafts, I finally had an email I was happy with. But I was too scared to send it. What if he ignored it? What if he shot me down? What if I got in trouble? I deliberated for a while, but eventually decided that, even if I was shouted at, I would at least know that I had tried. I held my breath, sent the email to him and waited. And waited. And waited some more. And then, once I was convinced I'd never hear back, I received a reply from his office manager, Lim La, asking if I had any time the next week to meet Ben to discuss the idea in more detail. Yes! Can you imagine! I was over the moon.

Our very first meeting was on a Thursday afternoon. I spent a bit of time preparing and even got an outfit out ready. And then, I forgot. I got home from school and opened up my emails to see a message from Lim La. It said, 'Hi Jeremiah, how far away are you? Your meeting with Ben started ten minutes ago.' I placed my head in both of my palms. I was embarrassed, petrified and angry with myself for throwing away such a golden opportunity. I wrote to Lim La and apologised. I think if I had been in Lim La's position I would have ignored my message. I could guess how busy someone like Ben was and to keep him waiting for so long was, for me, an unforgivable offence. But for some unknown reason, she decided to give me a second chance and simply rescheduled the meeting for the following week. There are a few people I have met who have changed my life for the better and Lim La is one of those people. I'm forever grateful to her for not giving up on me.

The night before I was due to meet Ben, I stayed up late, working on my pitch. All day I ran through the script in my head, silently rehearsing for the meeting, so I wouldn't make a misstep. Finally the moment came. I walked into New Broadcasting House and was escorted into the Radio 1 playlist room by Claire, the veteran receptionist. After a few minutes Ben walked in and shook my hand. There I was, age fifteen, in a suit that was a size too big for me, with my rickety black laptop patched together with tape, sat next to the boss of the radio stations I loved. I began my pitch and we had a long conversation about the direction of radio, as well as the work Ben wanted to do at Radio 1 and 1Xtra. I thought I had done reasonably well (I had made it on time at least) and left the building feeling on top of the world, eager to get started.

A few weeks went by and I didn't hear anything back. I am no good at waiting. I didn't chase Lim La, because I didn't want to put her to any more trouble. At a certain point, tired of checking my emails, I started to believe that my pitch was no good. What was I thinking, contacting the controller of Radio 1? As disheartening and deflating as the thought was, it gave me some closure at least, so I started to think about what I could do next. And then, one Friday afternoon, I was at my friend Henry's house playing *Call of Duty* on the PlayStation, when I received a call from a random landline. I picked up. It was the outreach manager from Radio 1. I jumped up, frantically gesturing at Henry to lower the volume of the TV. I was prepared to hear bad news. Luckily for me, it was the opposite.

Congratulations, she said. Everyone at the BBC was very impressed with my idea and they wanted to get the ball rolling. She asked me if I was happy to become the founder of the Radio 1 Youth Council and said that they were thinking of announcing the initiative at their annual press conference in a few weeks' time. I think I managed to squeak out a 'yes', before I hung up. I spent the next half an hour jumping around the room with Henry. I decided then and there that I would never expect the worst. I was elated but, weirdly, it made me think even harder about what I would have done if they had said no. A friend had said some wise words just a few days before: it's not a question of winning and losing, it's a question of winning and learning.

The next couple of weeks were a blur of meetings, briefings, workshops and one-on-one sessions with various important people at the BBC. And then came the announcement, accompanied by a full-page profile in a national newspaper. The headline read: 'Radio 1: "Teen Hero" head of Youth Council called in to help boss Ben Cooper (44) bridge the generation gap'.

I had the opportunity to visit the BBC over the next few weeks to help them scope out how the actual youth council would look. We then worked together to select a group of thirteen amazing young people from all over the UK. These young people had previously engaged with the BBC through work experience, their outreach programmes or events. Finally, in mid-2016, we hosted our first ever youth council meeting.

I couldn't believe that an idea I had put down on paper had actually come to life. I had never experienced anything like it before and kept grinning the whole way through the meeting.

Beyond the project itself, I had also created a new family of incredible young people who all shared similar interests. Out of this group, I created some friendships for life. Joel Borquaye, who had previously had the opportunity to do a work experience placement at the BBC. Ore who was scouted via work experience, alongside Jaguar, who was also building up her dance and techno DJ career. And how could I ever forget Naomi, the Welsh bashment queen whose extensive knowledge of dancehall and reggae would blow anyone away.

Every time we had a youth council meeting, we were presented with a new problem by a different department, from marketing to programmes or even outreach, with the aim of each meeting concluding with a solution. We had the opportunity to present new ideas for the Radio 1 Big Weekend, at one time the biggest free ticketed music event in Europe. We helped build up the #1millionhours campaign: kicking off on 1 December with the first drive in the lead-up to Christmas and running throughout 2016, the stations shone a spotlight on all things volunteering, in a bid to highlight the benefits of volunteering for young people. We were even given the opportunity to feature in an advert for Radio 1 that was aired on TV with Jaguar as our leading girl.

The youth council was a huge success. It showed me that I had a voice and that my ideas were valid. Looking back, it is scary to think that it almost didn't happen because I was too afraid to press 'Send'.

*

Karl

I first knew Pastor Mimi as Aunty Mimi. Her son was in my school. We used to go to each other's houses, eat, play. Our families knew each other. She also ran a Saturday school that I used to go to, learning literacy and numeracy.

Over time, me and her son started to follow a darker path. Gangs. She began to see me as the corruptor of her child. As a mother or father, you protect your investment! My parents did the same, whenever someone they didn't like came round. Every time Aunty Mimi saw me knocking at the door, her heart flipped.

Through her school, she was also reaching out to gang members, trying to engage them in conversation, attempting to steer them away from crime and towards God. Not Aunty Mimi any more, but Pastor Mimi. She counselled young boys and was managing to get through to them. She converted one of our friends and I immediately started to pay attention. I wasn't interested in changing my life at that point, but I was curious. I'm naturally curious. But I soon found that I was getting something from our conversations. After every chat I felt a lot better, just being able to speak to somebody.

She differentiates between a person and their actions. She believes that you are who you are and you do what you do. Two separate things. She would also say, 'You are not gangsters. You are young men who have made some bad decisions, who have received the ideology of "gangsterism". It's the ism that is leading you down the wrong path.' The more we talked, the more I told her. She could have sent me to prison if she wanted to, but she didn't. A bond was formed. I trusted her. I opened myself up to her. It got to the point where she wasn't just encouraging me or prompting me to talk, but was actually someone I saw as an advisor. Even if my question was, 'What do you think I should do? Should I put a hole in this person?' Her answer was always no, of course, but I began to listen to her. I was able to reflect on my worldview and on the damage I was doing. She created that space for me to think and reflect. My idea of winning began to change. We were top of the street league, but no one knew about the street league. The street league suddenly meant nothing. I realised that we were losing.

Losing sleep, losing peace, losing time, losing friends, losing sanity.

I eventually moved in with her. She opened her home to me and to a lot of my friends, creating a kind of informal gang rehabilitation hub. She didn't have a big house either. There were seven of us boys in one room, top to tail! It was a space for reflection, for healing. For hope, reformation and transformation.

I believe in something called the butterfly effect. The idea that a butterfly flapping its wings on one side of the planet can cause a hurricane on the other side. Without Pastor Mimi, I would not be where I am. And when I renounced gangsterism, a lot of people followed me. Without Pastor Mimi, I would be one of four things today: a criminal, in prison, insane or I would be dead. Simple as that.

The other person who had an enormous impact on my life was Asher Senator. He ran an organisation called C.O.D.E. 7 and let me use his studio for many years. He gave me a focus when it came to making music. Asher was a musician who had enjoyed a level of success in the 1980s with Smiley Culture. He was always clean dressed, in a suit. He was not a tall man, but he seemed like a giant. If Asher walked into a room, you would know about it. He was always chipper. Always smiling, always taking the time to greet everyone and make everyone feel welcome. A presence. If Pastor Mimi taught me about my heart and my mind, Asher taught me how to move. He taught me how to manoeuvre in the world.

He also taught me a few basics. When I knew him, he was spending a lot of time raising funds for his youth organisations. He showed me that it's one thing to have an idea, and another thing to make it happen. You need to think of the basics.

He also introduced me to John Kerridge, Assistant Director for Lambeth at the time. John's a good guy. A clean-hearted public servant. Initially, he was helping me to write the book of my life. He bought me my first Dictaphone. We built a relationship and used to meet once every couple of weeks at an Indian restaurant in Clapham. It was the best spot, one of those if-you-know-you-know places. Nothing more than a house. But over those conversations, he helped me to build up my confidence. He allowed me to picture a different future for myself.

And so then John introduced me to Camila Batmanghelidjh at Kids Company. Camila was a huge figure in my life – a tireless community organiser. She worked every single day. We used to meet up on a Sunday morning. Kids Company was one of the only charities that was felt at ground level. I take my hat off to her, to this day. She helped to mentor me, introduced me to people, showed me how to get things done.

And the late Tessa Jowell too. She believed in my voice. She believed that other people needed to hear what I had to say. She sent me on a course on broad-based community organising which changed my life. There was a session called 'Relational Power', which showed me the power of networking, the power of relationships, and how people can help you to incubate your ideas and make manifest your objectives. I took the principles of that course and injected it into my life like steroids. I was having forty or fifty meetings a week.

A by-product of the streets is that everyone is humanised. Everyone is the same. Violence does that. Because no matter what someone is wearing, what status they have or how protected they feel, they are still human. They will still have the same nine night, if you know what I mean. They will all have the same burial.

For years, because my currency was violence, I was never star-struck. I'd seen untouchable street dons disappear. I knew everyone was vulnerable. Everyone has to die. At a very basic level, it's not a strange concept. Everyone's the same. I also believe that people have more in common with their fellow human beings than they have points of difference. We have the same fears, anxieties, loves, wants. We have the same bodies. I always understood that fundamental point. I was also confident in who I was. I knew that I was an asset on any team. I could make a contribution to any conversation. I never doubted that. So whenever I met people, they weren't meeting Karl Lokko, some unknown. They were meeting that confidence. It was the same with everyone. From billionaires to buskers.

*

Lesson Three: Persevere

After a successful eighteen months helping to run the youth council, my time came to an end. I was struggling to balance my schoolwork with my other commitments (the extra-curricular activities didn't stop just because I was working with the BBC, trust me). But instead of an end, it became the beginning of something else. During my time with the youth council, I was told by a lot of people that I should take the project outside of the BBC and create a business. The idea was simple. Companies and institutions across the country were failing to understand and reach young people. They were not looking to young people for answers, they were spending huge sums of money on market research and advertising campaigns. It seemed crazy to me. Surely there must be some way to connect the two groups? The problem was, I didn't know where to start. As I mentioned earlier, I had never learned any practical business skills at school and I didn't know anyone I could speak to about taking the idea forward. I mean, how do you set up a business, age seventeen? However, despite my lack of knowledge, I decided to see what I could do to get the idea going.

I went back to my battered laptop and started researching the leadership teams of big companies. It seemed like the easiest step would be to email CEOs and COOs to tell them about the work I had been doing at the BBC, to see if they would be interested in discussing a similar set-up within their own companies. Tracking down email addresses is not easy, but I became an expert at it, spending hours browsing the web for clues and details.

I spent a few weeks slowly building up a database, carefully drafted an email listing my recent accomplishments and the achievements of the youth council, and personalised each one. When I had about forty perfect emails in my drafts folder, I hit send and sat back, feeling pleased with myself. The next day I opened up my inbox, talking myself up in the way that you do when you're waiting for good news. 'Maybe I'll find twenty replies? It was a good message after all. Actually, no. Let's say fifteen. I don't want to get too gassed.' Finally the page loaded: zero responses. Not even an acknowledgement email. This was disheartening. Following my previous experience, I refused to be defeated by it and just thought that I needed to go back to the drawing board and think up a better idea.

Daryl came round that night and I told him about my lack of success. On the wall of my room was a framed letter from the then prime minister David Cameron, commending me for the work I had been doing in the community.

Daryl pointed at it. 'Bro, you've got a letter from the prime minister in your room. You're seventeen. Never doubt yourself.'

I explained to him that maybe I just needed a new approach.

Daryl shook his head. 'If you stop sending emails, the possibility of a response is still zero. If you send one more, you've got another chance. The more you send, the more chances you'll have.'

He was right; all I had to do was keep going. I knew my business idea was sound; all I had to do was find a way to make contact with my target clients. I had the skills, knowledge and experience to succeed, so it was up to me to make the next step. I kept going. While continuing my search, I'd come across the email address of the CEO of Rolls-Royce Holdings, Warren East. I'd decided not to send him an email, as I wasn't sure how much a luxury car company would care about young people. Still, it was worth a try. I spent a day or two researching the company and drafted a new email:

Dear Mr Warren East,

My name is Jeremiah Emmanuel, I am a seventeen-year-old youth influencer and campaigner from London. Over the past six years I have worked with hundreds of young people in various different sectors and I have built up an understanding of how to drive engagement, reach target audiences and create conversations.

Last year I founded the BBC Radio 1/1Xtra Youth Council, this was because I identified a gap between the BBC and their target audiences. Since its birth, the stations have both been given advice on live events, content and shows, and now have a greater understanding of how to reach young people. Since then I have gone on to work with dozens of companies who have also wanted to achieve the same goals as the BBC.

I think Rolls-Royce would benefit from the advice of a similar group. I believe in youth and community engagement, and what could be better than having a greater insight into the minds of young people through a group of 'youth experts'.

It would be great if I could start a conversation with Rolls-Royce about such a group as I believe it could have a massive impact on the way you work with young people.

Please find below some links about the youth council and also what David Cameron had to say about my community work.

Kind regards,
Jeremiah

The next morning, I opened up my emails again, expecting a zero, but saw an email from Warren East in my inbox. A response from the CEO of Rolls-Royce Holdings:

Jeremiah

I have forwarded your email to the appropriate person in Rolls-Royce.

Thanks for making contact.

Copied in was the global head of community engagement for Rolls-Royce, Paul Broadhead. And the rest was history. I was ecstatic. After a few meetings at their corporate head office at Buckingham Gate in London, we got to work.

The company was trying to understand why only 3 per cent of work experience applicants were from BAME backgrounds. I organised focus groups with young people from Birmingham and Derby. Participants looked at facets of the company's branding, register, social media content, website interface, marketing materials and more to see if there were any obvious barriers to entry for people of minority backgrounds. Rather than it being a problem pushed back on potential applicants, we helped the company to see that they needed to do more to ensure their schemes attracted people from all backgrounds. Together we came up with a new set of criteria for the company to consider to help increase the number of applicants from BAME backgrounds, and asked our participants to present our findings back to the company. It was a success. Rolls-Royce, one of the most prestigious and exclusive brands in the world, listened to us. My company was born.

*

Lesson Four: Adapt

In 2016, the year I created my company, 663,615 other new businesses were registered across the UK. In the same year, 328,000 businesses collapsed. It's been stated that 30 per cent of new businesses fail within their first two years. The odds are scary. I didn't know how slim my chances were when I first set up my business, but then, I didn't really know much about business. Again, I turned to my trusty laptop. I discovered that the government did, at one stage, have various schemes to help support new businesses (the business growth service, most notably). However, like many of the services that allowed young people from disadvantaged backgrounds to access the opportunities that they are otherwise denied, most were closed in early 2016 as part of a broader range of budget cuts at the Department for Business, Innovation and Skills. So school was no help, my family couldn't help me (although they tried) and the government had nothing to offer. In the end, it was a friend of the family who provided the solution, allowing my idea to be housed as a company within his own, with invaluable support and assistance provided about the nitty-gritty details of fund-raising, organising payrolls, paying taxes and all the things you wouldn't really have a clue about as a teenager with limited business experience. The plan was for us to start out as a small part of a much bigger company and see if we could make it on our own after a year or two.

With the structures sorted, all that was left was to work out what we needed to do to make ourselves successful, to provide a service that companies would actually want. My experience with Rolls Royce gave me a confidence that my company offered something that was needed. I quickly realised, however, that it was not going to be possible to replicate the same model for business after business. Each company we worked with had their own specific ethos, their own specific customer base and their own culture and traditions to work within. We needed to be flexible, but we also needed a simple way to achieve our objectives without rewriting the rule book every other week.

More than anything, I knew that young people were the foundation of our work and our reason for being. That meant providing a platform for young voices was our primary goal, but we also had to find a way to ensure that these voices would be heard and under-stood. Once we were clear on our mission, we could create a blueprint to inform our work going for-ward. As with all of our projects, we spoke to the young people we worked with and managed to distil our programme down to three key elements that could be rolled out and reworked with every new client.

We knew that, whatever we did, it had to include young people. We worked hard to expand our network of young people across the UK and developed a new focus-group model that could be tailored to the needs and aims of individual companies. The focus groups were not what you might imagine: awkward conversations over lukewarm cups of coffee in fluorescent-lit meeting rooms. Our focus groups were designed to prompt maximum conversation, with staff members facilitat-ing and recording conversations and giving everyone around the table an opportunity to speak and be heard. We stepped away from traditional settings and gave the members of each group additional roles and responsibilities to ensure that they never strayed too far from our objectives. We needed a way to directly access the insight and experience of young people and our new groups provided that.

More than individual groups, however, we knew that if young people were to be a permanent factor in the decisions of a company, they needed to be able to provide input more than once every few years. We helped establish youth advisory boards – groups of young people employed by each company on a permanent basis – who were provided with a clear remit for ongoing and future work and were on hand to help tackle any questions that arose.

We also knew the benefits of speaking to individual members of staff and dismantling some of the limits of hierarchy. We created a reverse mentoring programme in which senior members of staff were advised by trained company contacts or junior members of staff, allowing space for fresh perspectives and new ideas to flourish. Of the three core practices, reverse-mentoring has proven the most popular and most successful; our network of reverse-mentors now includes schools, charities, companies and youth groups from across the UK.

One of the first organisations we worked with was the Queen's Commonwealth Trust, the Queen's official charity, established to champion, connect and fund young leaders who are 'working hard to change the world'. The charity was already doing some extraordinary work, but wanted to learn more about what a new generation felt about the social and environmental issues that affect (and divide) the world today.

We also worked with Superdry, to try and help them to reach a younger audience. That was a lot of fun. The groups we brought together were tasked with rethinking the company's marketing strategy; participants were introduced to new lines of clothes that were soon to be released and asked to create a quick campaign to target young people. With a new perspective came a fundamental shift in our understanding of the brand, and a lot of new ideas. These mini-campaigns were fed back and helped inform Superdry's future strategy.

We worked with Nando's on an exciting reverse mentoring project, connecting a group of young people from across London with the Nando's senior leadership team. We provided all of the young people with training prior to the session so they went in equipped with the right skills necessary for both sides to benefit. The aim of the project was to allow the executives to absorb the opinions of the young people and implement them in future projects, while the young people benefited from having the opportunity to make lasting contacts as well as getting the chance to receive feedback from a top person in their field of interest for free simply by participating in this unique experience. The initial meeting took place in the secret kitchen used by Nando's to test their new creations, where the young people and executives were able to meet for the first time and begin to talk. It was the start of a six-month journey, in which my company helped facilitate and expand the conversations taking place, ensuring that both mentors and mentees had a productive, rewarding and, most importantly, valuable experience.

We established a youth board at Parlophone record label to provide a direct link between senior music executives and the audience they were trying to reach. I will always remember our first meeting, where the new youth board members played the veteran industry figures samples of their personal playlists. Of all the creative industries, the music business is without question one of the most opaque and difficult to access. Our youth board helped to open up Parlophone in new ways, providing an essential sounding board and a source of advice on a variety of questions.

These were some of our early successes, but there were also many failures. Many unreturned calls and emails, many miscommunications, many promising leads that took us nowhere. But we persisted and adapted and, by the end of our second year, we had a roster of over a dozen major clients and were growing rapidly.

Like so much of my success, luck played a major part in the process, but I also had to work with what I had. I didn't know much. What I did know was what I liked and what other young people liked. I had the self-belief that Jamal Edwards had emphasised and the support of friends like Daryl who were honest with me. I also knew never to give up.

*

Karl

We think to dream is an achievement in itself. The reality is that we are not starting from zero. We're starting from minus ten, minus twenty, minus thirty. To scale the negative to get to the positive is huge. The possibility of failure feels much greater than the possibility of success. Moving up and out of my old life felt like walking along a tightrope. And when I got to the other side, there was still wonder at how the rope had managed to hold my weight. Still a risk of falling back in various ways.

God is my life. I know that the Creator has deemed me valuable. That simple fact gives me peace. It gives me confidence. If I'm ever feeling nervous, anxious or uncertain, I have a conversation with my Maker and the fears fade away. I am able to do whatever it is I have to do. It helps to keep things in perspective. It helps to keep me humble too. A lot of my humility comes from my knowledge that I am a creation. I was created. It is that humility and that grace that allow me to succeed.

Biblical stories are not just stories for me. I was David and the world was Goliath. All I had were stones. When I was sending out emails, looking for opportunities, in my lowest moments, those emails were my stones. That's how I live my life.

My story starts with weakness. I was getting robbed and I no longer wanted to be robbed. So I joined together with other boys who were getting robbed. We had a bit of strength together and we also had company in our misery. There was a formula. If you had your eyes open, you could easily see others who looked like you. Who looked like the kind of people you needed. I was kicked out of college on my first day. When I tried to get back in, I was told that I needed to achieve distinctions in my work in order to stay. So I knew I had to surround myself with people who were getting distinctions. The distinctioneers! And I found them. And we got distinctions.

*

Lesson Five: Give Back

Despite all of the barriers to entry, entrepreneurship has always appealed to me. This career path will not appeal to everyone but that's a good thing. There are amazing people who I've had the opportunity to work with simply because they are employees of a company and I myself value the hard work put in by my team. At the same time, I believe entrepreneurship encourages innovation. If I hadn't pushed through and set up my company, which we went on to call EMNL, Rolls-Royce may not have improved their engagement with prospective employees from BAME backgrounds. Nor would Nike global footwear execs from Portland, Oregon, have had the opportunity to take part in a speed-dating session with youths from London's inner-city communities, and gain authentic insight into their largest consumer demographic in the UK. Business, at its best, is all about helping people and I make sure that my business helps the people who are important to me.

When we execute our ideas, it is not only us who are able to benefit. In doing what I was passionate about, it was not only these larger businesses that benefitted, it was also a number of individuals. For instance, 60 per cent of the Radio 1 and 1Xtra Youth Council went on to find jobs within the BBC and that is before we were even a business. At Rolls-Royce, having a more diverse intake for interns led to a more diverse workforce and a better business, I believe. In everything I've done, I've tried to provide what I wanted when I was younger—an opportunity to broaden my horizons and learn from different people. That's all.

According to official figures, entrepreneurship in the UK is declining, but it should be on the rise. In 2018, there were 381,000 new businesses registered and 336,000 businesses that closed. I believe Generation Z is the most entrepreneurial in history. In my view, as the next generation of consumers, we expect more from businesses in terms of their commitment to making a positive impact culturally, environmentally and socially. We are used to working for our success and don't expect things to be handed to us on a plate. We know we have to be more creative, more industrious and more dedicated than ever before, if we are to achieve our goals. We need to find new ways to encourage entrepreneurship among a younger generation and help young people transform good ideas into a better reality. Most importantly, we need to change our view of what a businessperson looks like.

As I mentioned at the start of the chapter, my conversation with Karl in Brixton on that Saturday morning eventually led to an idea. Between us, we knew so many talented, intelligent, creative individuals who were lacking the experience, qualifications or contacts to get a

foot in the door of the industries they were most interested in. We knew some incredible designers, analysts,
entrepreneurs, publicists and marketers, who were all
known by a different name. Karl started talking about a
couple of boys who had been in the gang with him. He
put the word 'gang' in air quotation marks, saying that
it was really just a group of his best friends from school.
These boys were not thugs, criminals or predators – they
were simply young people who had limited options and
enough strength in their unity to make money and
wield influence. He talked about how unknown the
gang was when they started and how amazed he was,
after a few months, to hear boys in a completely different part of London talk about the gang with fear. That
was marketing at its best, surely? We laughed, but he
had a point.

And now we had a chance to keep the door open for
them. We started writing up a list and scribbled a title
at its top – 'The Hidden Alumni' – a small part of an
entire wave of disenfranchised young people who we
thought we could help. If there is anything I've learned
about business, it's this – make sure you give as much as
you get.

6

Politics

'If you don't do politics, politics will do you.'

Mike Sani

For a long time, when I was younger, I had two main career ambitions: become an artist or become prime minister. That was it. I wanted to help people and make a difference in the world, so prime minister seemed like a good option. But I was also obsessed with art: drawing, painting, reading books on artists and, best of all, visiting art galleries. Growing up in London, I used to visit galleries with my mum, whenever she had time (which wasn't very often), and also with my school. My two favourite galleries were (and still are) the Tate Modern and the National Gallery. There was something about being allowed to study these extraordinary paintings

and sculptures up close – some of which I'd seen repli-
cated hundreds of times on T-shirts, postcards and on
television – that I found inspiring. I never got tired of it.
While the rest of my class wandered off, flicking through
books in the gift shop or chatting, I'd be found standing
transfixed in front of a painting, soaking it up as best I
could before moving on to the next. The thing I also
found inspiring about the gallery trips was the fact that
we could just walk in and see these artworks for free. No
tickets, no queues, no questions, nothing. Just walk in.

One of our good family friends, Rebecca, was a successful
artist, and someone I got to spend a bit of time with growing up. I loved sitting in her studio watching her work,
observing how her projects progressed, from sketches to
early drafts to finished paintings. Rebecca also helped me
with my homework and gave me one-on-one painting
lessons (I was awful). One Thursday afternoon, when I
was about twelve or so, my mum took me over to her studio after school. When we arrived, Rebecca met us at the
door and explained that there were a couple of prospective buyers looking at her work, the owners of a large
national restaurant chain. We walked in and saw a man
and a woman – middle-aged, casually dressed – staring at
a few paintings that had been propped up against a wall.

Rebecca introduced my mum and then said, 'And this
is Jeremiah. One day he's going to be an artist or the
prime minister.'

The woman smiled, and said. 'Oh, that's good to hear.' Then she turned to me: 'Prime minister of which country?'

I looked at her in confusion. 'Um . . . Great Britain?'

There was a bit of an awkward silence and Rebecca took us into her kitchen and sat us down. My mum was furious. Shortly afterwards, Rebecca came back in. The couple had gone, she said. She wouldn't be selling them any paintings.

My mum and Rebecca talked for a while and I started to draw. I wasn't sure what had just happened. Did the woman think that I wasn't British? Or did she think that I couldn't be prime minister? I didn't know why she had said it, but I knew it had something to do with the colour of my skin. Up until that point, I had really believed that I could be prime minister, if I wanted to and if I worked hard enough. I believed I had the same chances as everybody else. All of a sudden, that belief was gone. Was I stupid to think that I could be involved in politics? Was there any possibility of me, Jeremiah, making any difference to the world around me? Could anyone who looked like me make a difference?

Fast-forward a few years, and I was having a similar conversation with my careers advisor at school. I had dialled down my ambitions by this point, thinking that maybe I could become a local counsellor or even an MP. I was told to think again. I was told that politics is a hard industry to break into and that I should really set my targets a little lower. I had never met the careers advisor before. He knew nothing about me, other than what I had told him. But that didn't stop him from making a decision about my future.

The responses I got are what I think a lot of young people expect to hear: you could never be prime minister; politics is not for you; there is no way you could make a difference. I feel sorry for anyone who thinks that way. I feel sorry for twelve-year-old me. I wish I could sit down with him now and try to explain things. I wish I could write him a letter.

*

You don't have to be a politician to influence politics. That's the first thing you've got to understand.

I was four years old when I attended my first campaign meeting. It was run by the Nelson Mandela School Foundation. This was a group set up by concerned parents within my community in south London. At that moment in time, in the early 2000s, the problems that young people in Lambeth faced were manifold, but no one seemed to be interested in listening to parents' worries, let alone attempting to address them, so a group got together to do something about it. The most pressing issue, as they saw it, was education. When I was five, the majority of pupils at secondary schools in the area were achieving fewer than five GCSEs at grades A* to C. It was a crisis. There was an increasing amount of violence between schools. It got so bad that some local parents didn't want to send their children to schools in the borough. But what was worse was the fact that even if you did, the chances of getting a place were slim. Not only were Lambeth's schools underperforming, but they were chronically oversubscribed, especially in Brixton. This meant that many young people living in the area had to travel a long way each day to get to school.

My mother joined the campaign after being approached by a few involved parents at the gates of my primary school. It might not be a concern for her at that moment in time, they argued, but it soon would be. She agreed immediately. She shared the views and concerns of those in the group. She wanted her three children to have the best education possible, so even though none of us had yet reached secondary school, this mattered. My brother remembers overhearing a conversation between my mum and her friend Sarah one afternoon. We were sitting on the floor in our living room playing Snake on my mum's Nokia phone. He remembers my mum saying something like, 'Will our children ever get the education they deserve? They are set up to fail before their lives have even begun.'

I didn't understand how important this statement was, but I knew they were passionate about the cause. The chair of the foundation was a lady called Ms Alison; she was joined by a board of trustees and a large campaign group. We would meet regularly, with meetings held in Brixton Hill at Ms Alison's home.

At this point, you might be wondering what the connection to Nelson Mandela was. When the group was founded they decided the future school needed a name. And what better name than Nelson Mandela? It was an opportunity to honour one of the twentieth century's great leaders, and a chance to inspire every pupil who would study there. I agreed, at the age of four. Mandela was a huge inspiration to me.

My mum had told me about the struggle within South Africa and the toxic racist roots of Apartheid, the system that oppressed so many people who looked like me. What I couldn't understand is why people were seen as less simply due to the colour of their skin.

Unfortunately, I began to learn what racism was at a very young age. There were a few moments that made me think I was different, in some way, but it was only when we took a trip to Scotland, not long before the school campaign began, that I realised what being 'different' meant. I'm sorry for yet another detour, but I think this one is important.

One summer, in 2005 I think, we took a very rare holiday to go and visit my mum's close friend Aunty Emma and her daughter Sally. This was the first time I had travelled outside of London and I was excited by everything I saw. We took a train up to Scotland and I was glued to the window for the whole journey. When we finally arrived we picked up our bags and walked out of the station to get to Aunty Emma's house. Eventually a bus arrived. It was already close to full, so we had to walk up to the top deck to find seats. I was in front of my family and walked towards the middle of the bus, where a group of teenagers sat, laughing and shouting. A few of them had big cans of beer in their hands, I remember. I sat in an empty seat in the middle of the group, my mum sat two seats in front and my brother Elijah sat across from me. It was suddenly very quiet. I looked around and saw that the teenagers were all staring at me, with angry expressions on their faces. Out of nowhere, one of the girls shouted out, 'Don't sit next to me, you nigger!'

I didn't know what to do. My mother turned around in disbelief and immediately started screaming at the group. I felt hurt, upset and confused. I didn't know these people. Why were they being so horrible to me? It was my first real experience of racism, but it wasn't the last. Thankfully, I was lucky enough to be surrounded by people who always made sure to correct damaging stereotypes, reminding me of my value as a person and the beauty of my skin.

For me, and for many of my friends, Nelson Mandela was often put forward as a model to aspire to. He was someone who had changed the world for the better, someone who had turned hatred into peace, and someone who was respected and loved around the world. Like my mum and our family friends, Mandela reminded me of my value.

The Nelson Mandela School Foundation wanted to try something different. They wanted to instil a sense of responsibility and ambition in young people. They wanted young people in south London to follow in the footsteps of Mandela.

As a part of the campaign, all of the kids involved in the campaign created a scrapbook; I remember taking part in this. It was filled with our plans and our hopes for the school. While Mandela was on a visit to London, we attempted to deliver it to him but, due to unforeseen circumstances, this wasn't possible. We sent it off to him when he got back home instead. He sent a letter in return, full of joy and gratitude. It spurred us on. It was a sign that anything was possible. I was part of a group of children roped in to help advance the plans for the school. We met regularly in an attempt to get the plans moving. We started by lobbying the local authority (Lambeth Council). We used to attend the full council meetings and voice our concerns about education in the borough, setting out the case for why the school was needed. We would attend the meetings with high numbers of campaigners sitting in the public gallery, all of us armed with posters and leaflets.

We wrote to our local MP, Keith Hill, and went to see him at his constituency office and in Parliament. We felt we had to get across the desperate nature of our situation; we had to convince leaders and policy-makers like him that the school would benefit not only future students, but also the wider community. On one occasion, we went on a trip to lobby in Parliament once and I remember my mum touching the wall declaring that I would take my place in the building one day. Her prayers did come true when I later joined the UK Youth Parliament.

We got on to BBC news, talking about the school project. There is a video somewhere in the BBC archives of me marching arm-in-arm with my friends, singing a song we had made up for the campaign: 'We can work together. To build our school called Nelson Mandela.'

As the campaign gathered momentum, we learned that the Queen was due to officially open another new school in Clapham, Lambeth Academy. One of the first academies. We knew, even at that young age, that to get people's attention we had to do something provocative. We had to make an impact, in whatever way we could.

We saw the Queen's visit as an opportunity to make a statement. We came up with the idea of wearing bin bags, each with a letter on the front, spelling out 'ARE WE TRASH?' The point we were trying to make was that we felt as if we were being treated like rubbish. No one cared about us, no one listened to us. Lambeth Academy was a step in the right direction, but it wasn't enough.

So we took up our places near the school, along the route the Queen would take, with our bin bags and our leaflets, and we waited. Eventually we spotted the motorcade approaching and we saw the Queen staring out at us as she drove by. You can imagine the kind of questions she was asking: 'Why are there children dressed as rubbish protesting the opening of a new school?'

We had got attention. We had the community behind us. We had spoken to decision-makers We had even caused the Queen to frown. So was the campaign successful? Well, no. The Nelson Mandela School was never built. But the campaign gave us hope. And I like to think that it led to some small victories. There was, at the time, a broader schools redevelopment programme in place across the country and some of the local schools in Lambeth were selected to be a part of it. Although our school wasn't built, another new school in Brixton, the Evelyn Grace Academy, was – eventually. Our message had got through in some way. And, in fact, I was invited to speak at the school not long after it was opened.

*

Precious

I grew up in Brixton, south London. My first introduction to politics and the political process was witnessing my mother and neighbours raise questions about the number of syringes in the bushes around our local park in a Brixton Town Hall meeting when I was about four or five. I couldn't understand why everyone was shouting. I could see that there was a large group of unhappy and very vocal people (my mum and neighbours), and a smaller group of grumpy and very quiet people (the local counsellors). The power dynamic was obvious. The counsellors had all the power. All they had to do was endure the shouting and say something positive at the end. Notes were made, assurances were given that the problem would be 'looked into', but really, what else were they going to do?

I went to St Martin-in-the-Field, in Tulse Hill. I was very good at school. Exams were a challenge, but I always did well. I remember going home after I got my AS-levels results. My Dad took one look at my results, and said to me, 'Oxford or Cambridge?' It was interesting because he was the first person to ask. None of my teachers had ever thought Oxbridge might be a possibility. But when I went back to school, there was a renewed interest in me. There was talk of mentors, application preparation, away days. So I went up to a Cambridge for a taster day, and decided to go there. I worked hard, got the grades, and that was that.

My interest in politics really began at university. I had decided to study PPS, or politics, psychology and sociology. There were four or five black people on my course. But this was four or five out of 100 people. We used to get together a lot. One of the things that united us was the way race impacted our lives, that and class. The difficulty of studying politics at an institution like Cambridge is that our course was largely made up political theory from a particular perspective. Old, dead white men, in other words, who had nothing to do with me, and nothing to say about my world. People who had written about people like me as 'savages'. I mean, one of the libraries is named after one of the founding fathers of eugenics.

I wanted to get a broader understanding of the political process. I hadn't studied politics at all up to that point. But I was interested in politics – how societies organised themselves. How different groups come to common decisions and create laws. What are the mechanics of contemporary politics, and what are the theories behind particular viewpoints or parties? Why does the Conservative Party believe that the government should do less, and people should do more? Why does Labour (especially recently) have more of a socialist spin, in terms of the government should do more? Politicians by and large are from similar backgrounds and went to the same universities. So why do they have such different solutions to the same problems?

The town hall meeting taught me that politics was something that happened to me, a belief that was confirmed a few years later when I was planning to apply for university and was hit by politics in a particular way. My year was the first to have to pay increased tuition fees. The coalition government, and a deputy prime minister who had gained power on a promise to abolish tuition fees, had been part of the decision to raise them significantly. All of a sudden politics was a major part of my life. I was facing a £27,000 debt because of politics. A subject I had shown little interest in was suddenly having a huge bearing on my life. That's something I wish had been pointed out to me when I was younger – the ways in which politics shaped my life.

*

The school campaign was my first insight into politics, and it taught me a lot. I learned that individuals can

233

make a difference. I learned that if I wanted to help other people, I could. I learned how to get people to notice. And, even at a young age, I learned where power sits, at a local and at a national level.

For those who aren't as familiar with British politics, I'll quickly talk you through it. Let's begin with local government. I will use London as an example. We have thirty-two boroughs and thirty-two local author-ities. Each borough is split into wards, and each ward has its own councillor, who represents you. Your councillors and your local authority are responsible for the government activities specific to your area: social care, education, refuse collection, roadworks. In London we also have the Greater London Assem-bly, or GLA, overseen by the Mayor of London. The GLA is responsible for London-wide issues. Then you have central government, what you are most likely to imagine when you think of government or political power. Our central government is based in the Houses of Parliament in Westminster and is divided into two houses: the House of Commons, where our MPs sit, and the House of Lords.

One morning, about halfway through my final year of primary school, Chuka Umunna, then our newly elected local MP, came to give an assembly. I was sit-ting on a wooden bench at the side of the hall and wasn't paying much attention until he began to speak. He said that his family came from Nigeria and also that he had attended our primary school. He started to talk about his work as an MP. He described his constituency surgeries, where he spoke to local residents about issues they were facing. And he spoke about sitting in Parliament, where he could raise those issues on our behalf to the country's leader. He spoke about how important the local community was to him, about his passion for helping those who were in need of help. This was someone I recognised. His family came from Nigeria, just like mine did, and he had a funny-sounding name, just like me. He even looked a bit like me. I remember running up to him to shake his hand at the end of the assembly. I wanted his job, I wanted to influence change, I wanted to change lives, I wanted to be like him. My knowledge of politics at the time was not extensive enough to fully understand the mechanisms behind it. However, following the assembly, I began to stay in the loop with current affairs. Every morning I would watch the news, every afternoon I would read a newspaper, paying particular attention to anything that felt remotely connected to the world of politics.

The next year, in my first year at secondary school, I sat in an assembly listening to a presentation by Alex Goode, the youth coordinator from our local council. He was talking about the upcoming youth elections in my borough. The youth elections were held every year; it was an opportunity for young people to be elected into ceremonial roles. It was a chance to represent all of the young people in your borough, connect to decision-makers and amplify your voice. There were two roles available. As a Member of the Youth Parliament (MYP), you would be able to represent young people at the UK Youth Parliament. This was an independent youth organisation; you couldn't influence policy or laws, but you would have the opportunity to take over the House of Commons in Parliament in a televised TV debate. The second role was the Youth Mayor, a ceremonial position. Nonetheless, you could focus on issues at a local level, you would be able to shadow the Mayor of the borough and you would represent all young people in the area. More importantly, the council would provide you with a fund of £25,000, which you could use to give grants to local organisations and project ideas generated by young people.

I won't bore you with the details but eventually, after a lot of hard work, I was elected Youth Mayor, and later, a Member of Youth Parliament.

One of the first issues I had to tackle in Youth Parliament was the killing of Mark Duggan in north London and the ensuing riots of 2011. While travelling in a taxi, Mark Duggan had been pulled over by the police and shot dead by a police officer. He was unarmed, but his death was later declared lawful following an inquest. Immediately after Mark Duggan's shooting, riots evolved from peaceful protests, first in the local Tottenham area before spreading nationwide. The riots were about a collective feeling. They were an expression of anger and frustration with the establishment, and with a system that many felt had little regard or respect for their lives. This was in the midst of austerity measures, you have to remember, where community services and benefits were being slashed across the board. I remember walking through Brixton and Croydon and seeing shop windows smashed, buildings burning. The riots were used as an opportunity to loot and vandalise by some people. But that doesn't detract from the feelings that prompted them – a sense of anger, despair and hopelessness.

As well as the destruction, I also saw the local community coming together to help those who had lost their businesses or homes, to protect the neighbourhood. The media placed the blame squarely at the feet of young people, so it was my job as a Member of the Youth Parliament to try and correct that picture. My solution was to make a short documentary in which I interviewed different members in my community, from youth leaders to young people. I wanted to find out what their thoughts were about the state of London and what needed to be improved. I felt this was important because these were the voices that get rarely listened to. When we had finished the video, I shared it with my colleagues in the Youth Parliament and with local boroughs across London. It was a rare opportunity for young people to speak out, rather than be spoken for. And the responses I got back made me feel that we had gone some way to challenging the dominant narrative that was emerging. Young people were the future. We should try to understand the cause of their anger, rather than condemning a generation.

*

I spent a lot of time as a Member of the Youth Parliament exploring the key items of legislation and policy that affect young people. In some areas over the last few years, there has been some positive change. In 2014, the Children and Families Act and the Care Act were passed, which strengthened rights for young carers. The acts were largely driven by external groups and a large number of young people. The passion of young carers, and the passion of those charitable organisations that recognise and represent them, is inspiring to see and a reminder that hard work and perseverance does still pay off.

In 2017, the National Citizen Service (NCS) Act was also passed in Parliament, making the NCS programme officially recognised as a national youth scheme and expanding its future plans so that opportunities continue to grow for young people outside of main-stream education. Although it isn't nearly enough, it is a step in the right direction for youth opportunities, engagement and activism.

Politics has become incredibly frustrating to me, how-ever, because of the lack of movement on some of the most important issues affecting my community. Knife crime has very little high-impact government support; mental health support isn't recognised enough by some of the most important institutions; education policy is still incredibly outdated; poverty is only getting worse; and discrimination isn't getting any better. Essentially, so many of the issues I explore in this book aren't being given their due focus in the political world. That doesn't make them any less important, but they are treated as if they are.

The reasons for this vary. Politicians will often argue that the country cannot afford to invest properly in youth services, or that it's a 'cultural' problem that money won't address. Sadly, I think it is often just a case that the people in power have no understanding of the lives of people like me, and the struggles that exist in communities like mine. Two of the last three Prime Ministers went to Eton, Britain's most prestigious pri-vate boarding school, and then when on to Oxford University. Tory MPs, that is, those currently running our country, are six times more likely to have gone to private school than the general population. So can we really be surprised when the policies they prioritise aren't the ones that matter to young people in working neighbourhoods?

Ultimately, the issues our government and Parliament will prioritise depends on who's sitting at the table. If we don't want issues that affect young people and working-class communities to get overlooked, we need those people involved in decision making. Otherwise deep problems, many of which have viable solutions which have been worked through by people on the ground, and developed by talented people in the third sector, will be left undebated in Parliament, and often completely ignored. This is why youth engagement in politics is so important. We need people with a variety of experiences in Parliament to make sure that issues that matter for ordinary people, but not the privileged, aren't overshadowed.

During my time at the Youth Parliament I came to learn that there are a frightening number of damaging laws which deserve to be challenged, if not completely rewritten. Some of these have been ignored for literally hundreds of years! One example which I find particularly shocking is the Vagrancy Act, which was passed in 1824 but remains in place today. The Vagrancy Act criminalises homelessness, by making it illegal to sleep rough or beg. When people are in desperate situations the state should support them, not punish them! As, John Sparkes, the CEO of crisis has said : 'There are real solutions to resolving people's homelessness – arrest and prosecution are not among them'. How this law has remained in place for almost two hundred years beggars belief.

Homelessness is an example not just of us failing to move forward to correct an injustice, but where Britain has moved backwards. The government's own statistics show that homelessness has increased by 165 per cent since 2010, when the Tory and Liberal Democrat coalition came into power. Like with youth services, the government slashed the funding available to support the homeless, and the results can be seen by all. The homeless charity St Mungo's suggests that a major cause of this increase was changes to the benefit system, which left many people without sufficient income to keep a roof over their head. In addition, they say reduced access to support services, due to large cuts to local authorities, will likely have exacerbated the problem.

This is just one of many of the negative impacts of austerity, and I have covered others in previous chapters. We have to ask ourselves: What does it say about our political system and our politicians if the decisions made in parliament increase hardship and injustice, not work to support people who need it, and lay the groundwork for a fairer society?

Finally, I want to return to the issue of youth services and knife crime to demonstrate how, even when they try to address a problem, our politicians can get it dramatically wrong. As I have said earlier, I think a large reasons for the increase in knife crime we have seen in London is because our young people lack sufficient opportunity, a problem which has been worse by cuts to youth clubs and youth services. However, what bright idea do you think the government had to correct the problem? A hashtag campaign on chicken boxes.

That's right. In August 2019, the Home Office spent £57,000 printing 321,000 chicken boxes, which they distributed to chicken shops to put their meals in. The boxes had the hashtag #KnifeFree on the outside, and on the inside showed stories of young people who had chosen to pursue positive activities instead of engaging in knife crime. The campaign was, rightly in my view, called out as patronising, inadequate and borderline racist. It's just one example of the lazy approach government so often has to the problems which afflict, and which they have inflicted, on communities unlike their own.

*

If we think about some of the biggest political issues of the day – healthcare, education, foreign policy and (sorry to say it) Brexit – it's clear that there is a growing divide between young and old. Is this a moment to silence a new generation or is it a moment to empower them?

One of the biggest issues that we looked at within the Youth Parliament was the question of voting age. In fact, the majority of participants (myself included) worked to make the issue our national campaign goal on several occasions. We were not the only ones. For years, some Members of Parliament have been bringing up the importance of offering the vote to young people at the ages of sixteen and seventeen, arguing that, in today's world, young people are much better positioned to understand the world of technology and how politics needs to change with the times.

However, the issue never gained much traction. The Conservative-led governments over the last decade have consistently shot down these proposals. And previous governments never discussed making this a real possibility, usually by indirectly saying (or at the very least, making people think they meant to say) that young people aren't capable of the critical thinking and decision-making that it takes to handle the pressure of making an informed vote. At this point, that logic has largely been disproven; young people – as I touch on multiple times in this book – have proven on more than enough occasions that, in today's world, we can make decisions as well, if not better, than many adults.

Thankfully, despite sixteen- and seventeen-year-olds being held back by how slowly the times are changing for them, young people across the country are becoming increasingly clued up about the importance of being politically active. Beyond just voting, record numbers of young people are signing petitions, joining peaceful protests and starting campaigns that work with their local governments.

This all runs counter to a narrative that did the rounds a few years ago, that young people are apathetic or lazy. For example, immediately after the EU referendum in 2016, there were high-profile stories about young people failing to come out and vote. However, when pollsters like Opinium looked deeper into voting behaviour, they found 64 per cent of young people had taken part in the referendum, not far off the nationwide average. Moreover, I think when young people vote in lower proportions than older people, we shouldn't see this as a sign of apathy, but rather a failure of the political system to offer young people as real choice. This is especially the case because of Britain's first-past-the-post system, which means that not every vote counts. I believe young people are waking up to the importance of voting, partly due to the blow of Brexit, which most young people opposed. At the 2019 election it certainly seemed we'd learned our lesson. Over 4 million younger voters registered to vote in the run-up to the 2019 election. Regardless of how they voted, a greater level of political engagement is undoubtedly a good thing.

*

Precious

I find politics really frustrating but also really exciting.

Let's talk about the establishment. Politics is a game that anyone can win or lose, but only a select few people can play. Social media has democratised what it means to have influence. It has become easier to generate social capital, and to make noise on a local level, than ever before.

Look at the recent headlines about Boris Johnson's representative refusing to comment on whether or not Boris thinks black people are intellectually inferior. How can you refuse to comment on that? As much as the establishment is important, and does require people from our communities to infiltrate it, I worry about how big a difference can be made from the inside.

I think young people are becoming more and more politically active and engaged. That is to do with big-ticket issues like Brexit that have called into question whose interests are being served in the long and short term. Young people have access to more information than ever at an earlier stage and are globally connected, meaning we can see what is happening in other nations, and draw comparisons.

We need to do more in terms of engaging with views we do not like. It seems like there are a lot of echo chambers. People are choosing to follow and listen to people who share similar views to themselves and nothing changes. The conversations we are having need to go beyond social media. People need to attend surgeries with their MPs, in addition to watching Prime Minister's Questions. We have to do more to hold our leaders to account for the decisions they are making and the policies they are supporting. They are most responsive to those who wield voting power.

Look at the regeneration project in Brixton, which is essentially gentrification. What we've seen is that there are a lot of new housing developments being built, but only a small proportion are going to low-income families from the area, who might not necessarily be able to afford to buy or rent in the area otherwise. It's not just the property, either. A lot of these developments are built with so-called community spaces, available only to the private buyers or renters.

My godson, for example, lives in a council block where the only redevelopments have been new fire doors, installed in the wake of Grenfell. His parents, and many *of the residents have long been petitioning for a new play area for the children in the local playground, to no avail. Then one day, they discover that a fire pit is being built. Apparently the council was worried about residents barbecuing on their balconies. Fire safety is important but it seems they are more motivated by fear than actual community cohesion.*

The world is built on inequality. This country is built on foundations of slavery, and colonialism. To move on, we would really need to dismantle every institution and every organisation that has benefitted from slavery or colonialism in some capacity. We would need official apologies, we would need reparations. Has that happened in any way shape or form? No. Look at the state of the country. Look at the way that people are treated in school, or treated on the street. Look at the rise of racism.

I am speaking as someone who went to a very privileged institution and so I recognise I have a different perspective on what is possible. But I think real change can be achieved.

*

I believe in the power of political education. While in the UK Youth Parliament, a campaign that most of the MYPs were passionate about was creating a curriculum that prepared students for life. We as young people are blessed to have one of the most developed and-respected education systems in the world. However, a major aspect that is missing are lessons in how we proceed forward in life on a day-to-day basis. At school I was never taught about paying tax, building a good credit file, getting a mortgage, or even more practical skills, such as first aid, interpersonal skills or public speaking.

Politics is a subject that I believe needs to be taught to every pupil in every school, primary and secondary. Our political system is at the heart of everything we do. Laws and policies affect all areas of our lives. Without an understanding of how politics works, we are powerless to change it. Even worse, we don't care. In my secondary school, most of my friends were not taught about politics. They were not told how the country was run. A few people I knew couldn't have told you, aged fifteen or sixteen, who the prime minister was. These friends were not stupid. They were not told and simply did not care. But because they did not see a connection between Westminster and their lives, they were not interested.

When I joined Archbishop Tenison's School, my form tutor was an extraordinary teacher named Ms Gordon. She was someone who wanted the best for all of us. I had other inspiring teachers (as I've mentioned), but Ms Gordon stood apart in one crucial respect: she wanted us to understand how politics worked. In our form tutor sessions, once in a while we would learn about the political system in this country. This gave all of us an insight into how the government worked, and how to hold our local decision-makers to account. It made me understand the world around me, and how I could work to change it. It gave me agency in the world.

I believe politics should be a compulsory subject for all schoolchildren, from the earliest possible age. It's unfortunate that it can usually only be picked as a subject at A-level, and very rarely at GCSE level. Understanding how the political system works and how they can have a say is the best way to encourage young people to participate in the political process.

Of course, while young people might not know the details of how politics work, they can see its consequences. I grew up in a decade that saw funding to youth services cut by 70 per cent. That is politics in action. Faced with that reality, you can react with anger and participation or you can react with anger and indifference and the truth is, more often than not, young people are driven to the latter. So many of my friends believe that politicians do not care about them, their families or their areas. And they are right, most of the time. But refusing to participate in the political process is not the answer. The best way to express that anger is to get involved and help create positive change. It's easier than you think.

There a number of different organisations that push for this. I have been engaged with a few. After doing my research I signed up to join events and conferences. One of these is an amazing organisation called Bite the Ballot. Bite the Ballot pushed to get more young people involved in the political system. They drove thousands of young people to vote, and in 2015 were behind National Voter Registration day. The organisation was founded by Mike Sani, a former school teacher who was tired of the state of the political system and the fact that not enough young people were engaged. After getting involved with Bite the Ballot I participated in a number of their initiatives. This included a televised debate on ITV, in which I sat on a panel of young people. We got to question political leaders directly, holding them to account for their campaign promises. This saw me participate in a debate with Nigel Farage, the then leader of UKIP, and Nick Clegg, the then leader of the Liberal Democrats. I also took part in another debate in the lead-up to the EU referendum, where I had a discussion about the issue with the right-wing commentator Katie Hopkins. In every case, I gave as good as I got. Bite the Ballot has done some amazing work, I was glad to be a part of it. And all I had to do to get involved was to mention my interest and connect with them online.

I began this chapter by sharing a quote from Mike: 'If you don't do politics, politics will do you'. It's simple: if you do not engage with and in the political process, then politics might affect you in a negative way. To resist that, you can get involved on a grassroots level, similar to my family in the Nelson Mandela School Foundation campaign. Or if you're passionate about a particular issue you can sign up to become a member of an organisation that is leading the fight. The UK Youth Parliament was another way I got involved with the political system. It is open for anyone between the ages of eleven to eighteen to apply and is a great way to project your voice on a national platform. It also gave me a greater insight into the political process and allowed me to meet and learn from decision-makers.

And there's one more route to get involved in politics. Vote. Use your right to vote. If more young people voted in elections, every political party would have to base more of their campaign and manifestos around young people. At the moment, due to low turnouts of younger voters, parties don't seem too bothered on securing our votes. But if young people voted at the same rates as older voters, the whole political system would be turned on its head. Last but not least, it is important to hold your MP accountable. They represent you and everyone else in their constituencies. If you have any concerns or are passionate about a particular issue, write to them or go and see them at their local surgeries. Their voting on laws in Parliament is heavily based on what the residents in their constituencies want.

Finally, we need more and more young people to consider going into politics, especially those from working-class backgrounds and ethnic minorities. I do not feel Parliament totally represents us as a country in terms of diversity. We must continue to fight and work hard so more under-represented voices are heard within the walls of power.

*

Precious

Many people are limited by their environment and try to impose those limiting beliefs on others. This is why we have to get as much exposure as possible to alternative perspectives. The internet has helped greatly with this. Ultimately politics will affect your life whether you engage or not. But if you engage, you have an opportunity to be a part of the process and if you engage enough you can influence it.

Firstly, interact with your local MP. They work for you. If you really care about your area, know who they are, and what their record is, and what they have promised, and hold them to account.

If engaging directly with politicians is not for you, there are groups whether physical or digital that feel strongly about issues and are mobilising to affect change either via MPs or independently. Joining together with people who share similar views and taking action whether via a vote, creating a new scheme, or protesting is engaging with politics and it all make a difference. We can have more influence as a collective voice than individually.

*

I wonder what my life would have been like if more people had told me I could be prime minister when I was growing up. I am not saying it would help me to become prime minister, but maybe it would have given me more of a belief that I could make a difference. I wonder what would happen if all young people were taught about politics and told how they could do more for themselves and their communities. What would it cost to provide that self-belief? And what could it lead to? I sometimes think about what I would say to the twelve-year-old me who was told he couldn't be prime minister. Something like this, maybe:

Dear JE,

I hope you're keeping well!

I wanted to write this letter to you from the future to give you some advice. Keep being ambitious, keep dreaming and believing. You will find a way out of your current situation and hardships. Your environment does not define you. You can become whatever you want to become. Continue being optimistic; however, I want you to be aware of something.

As you know by now, your appearance, background and beliefs may work against you as you navigate this world. Any dreams or goals you may have will be harder to come by than for your counterparts from more privileged backgrounds. It's not fair, but it's the truth. But don't give up. I love your commitment and urgency to get involved in politics, I know one day you would love to be in a high position or even the prime minister. There is something I feel is important to share.

You will discover that there are three accepted routes to becoming prime minister. The most straightforward route is via Oxford or Cambridge University. Attending these universities were the starting points for almost every prime minister in history. If you want to go, great. First, you have to ensure you get the best exam results you can, so stay focused in school. You may have some help, but you can rely on no one else to get you there. A second route you can go down is attending a Russell Group university, like four prime ministers in history. If those routes do not work, you could maybe skip university. Five prime ministers in the history of this country didn't attend university. You have options.

It will be a challenge, life is a challenge. But I want you to know that even though you are at a disadvantage, you could create your own unique route to becoming a success. If you want to, you can become prime minister.

Don't give up on your dreams and goals. I have grown up to find out we live in a cruel world, but we do need leaders like you to bring solutions to the issues that affect our society.

I believe in you.

Kindest regards,
Jeremiah

7

Charity

One Christmas Eve, when I was around ten years old, my mum called me into the kitchen. She had to pop out to the shops, she said, and told me to keep an eye on the pans. 'Keep stirring,' she said. 'Make sure you don't let anything burn.' I loved cooking with my mum and thought of myself as a bit of a junior masterchef, so this was music to my ears. I worried about my mum, however. It was super cold that day and she had already been out to the shops three or four times already. There were a few more pans than usual, but this wasn't anything out of the ordinary. Each Christmas we would have a feast, a mix of traditional British options and

Nigerian cuisine – peppered chicken or turkey, roast potatoes, devils on horseback, jollof rice, egusi soup – and Mum would always make a start on Christmas Eve.

I stirred the pots and eventually my mother came home, laden with more bags. 'This year, we are not just cooking for us,' she said. That evening, she said, we were also going out to feed the homeless. She and a few of her friends were making thirty or forty meals each to hand out in central London. This was on top of her usual cooking for our Christmas feast.

It had been a difficult year. My mum had been in and out of hospital and we didn't have very much money, as she hadn't been able to work. It would have been perfectly acceptable for her to stay in and focus on herself and her family. But no. A few hours later, we were standing on a square near Holborn station, handing out cardboard containers of hot food to a long queue of homeless men and women. For her, this was what Christmas was all about. Despite the things that were going on at home, she was grateful. She felt 'blessed', she told me, and saw it as her duty to pass those blessings on. Driving home with her friends, singing Christmas carols, laughing and joking, I could see that we did have a lot to be thankful for. We were in a position to help and so we did.

This was nothing new. Just after I turned three, my mum set up her first ever community project. It was called

Beauty4Ashes. Her main objective was to get young people off the streets by providing them with practical skills and opening their eyes to the world around them. Some of the young people she worked with were either offenders or at risk of offending. Others were teenage mothers or young people not in full-time education or employment. She always brought me along, whether it was cookery classes, interview workshops, money management classes or trips to art galleries.

I feel like her compassion rubbed off on me. And that is what this chapter is about. Giving back. Growing up as I did in communities with clear divides along lines of race, wealth, gender and so much more, the most inspiring and exciting experiences for me were when I was working under, with and for organisations that inspired change and supported the growth and understanding of young people. I wasn't alone. In 2017 alone, 20.1 million people in the UK volunteered their time through a group, charity or organisation. It's a huge number, but I think it could be higher. Giving back doesn't necessarily mean working somewhere for free or putting your hand in your pocket. In this chapter I will be talking about the importance of helping others, regardless of the situation you find yourself in.

*

Victor

My name is Victor Acquah. I work in finance and cur-rently live in south London. I'm also an army officer.

I grew up near Clapham Common and moved to Brixton when I was about ten years old. I think when I moved to Brixton, it really opened my eyes to the challenges of being a young black man or black boy in an inner-city environ-ment. Being in Brixton, you're in a volatile environment where you have to be very alert and very sharp if you don't want to get sucked into the system. By the system, I mean the world of drugs, gangs and all the other unhealthy things that can happen in and around any inner-city areas.

My parents wanted me to go to Archbishop Tenison's School in Oval because it was a religious school and had a good reputation at the time. They thought they were sending me there to escape some of the problems of living in London but, in fact, school was where I found them. It was a tough school. It's where I got my education, in more ways than one.

There were a lot of fights and a lot of gang activity. Because of the school's location, kind of in the middle of a few areas, there were kids attending who were affiliated with a var-iety of gangs. We had the 28s, the Peckham Boys, the Ghetto Boys and one or two others. In that situation, it was almost impossible to opt out – sitting on the fence was a statement in itself and could lead to bullying. So I got together with the Brixton Boys, Stockwell Park and the 28s, because they represented the area I was living in. Back then gangs from the same area sort of got along. You didn't have that postcode rivalry. If you lived in Brixton, you were in the Brixton gangs. It didn't matter which really, as long as it was in Brixton. Your enemies weren't from Brixton – they were the gangs in Peckham or New Cross.

I was getting sucked into the system, but I was lucky enough to grow up at a time when there were lots of opportunities in the local area for me. A lot of youth clubs and youth initiatives, a lot of places generally open and available to young people in south London. These were places you could go to do your homework, to play pool or play on a computer, to buy a cheap meal. A sort of home away from home. A shelter from the streets. I started to go to a lot of youth centres after school with my friends and got to know the people running them quite well. I realised that a lot of them weren't paid. They weren't getting nearly enough money from the government to keep the centres open and well run. So many people there did it because they wanted to give back; they wanted to provide an alternative for young people in the area. They knew that talk wasn't enough. Action mattered. It planted a seed in me. I began to see that change really only comes about if you put in the effort. You can't sit back and wait for something good to happen.

I loved the youth clubs and the youth centres, but the one thing I was missing was structure. One day, I got talking to one of the older guys at a community centre, and he told me about the cadets. 'Come along,' he said. 'If you don't like it, you don't have to come back.' So I went. I remember being a little nervous. I was on my own and I wasn't sure what to expect. These are army guys, yeah? What's going to happen? Are they just going to shout at me and make me do press-ups for an hour?

In some ways, it was exactly like I expected, but in others, it was nothing like that. There was a lot of marching and saluting and plenty of sharp uniforms. But there was no shouting. Everyone was kind. The best way to describe it is as a family. No one really knew me, but I was immediately welcomed in. People took the time to speak to me, and understand a bit about me. I got to watch what went on and I liked a lot of what I saw.

The first thing I was taught was the value of teamwork. As an individual, there's only so much you can do. In a team, you're strong. It connected a lot to what I was seeing at school – the need to join up to a gang for security. At cadets, it was something else. We were also taught about community work. For example, you know from a young age that if you see an old lady walking across the road, you should help her. It's about the benefit that you as an individual can give to somebody else, without demanding something in return. After my first few cadet sessions, I used to wish I could see an old lady in trouble, just so I could run over and help her.

It wasn't all being a goody-goody. It was assault courses, map-reading, strategy and leadership workshops. I was moving out of my comfort zone and I thrived. The cadets became a very solid thing in my life at a time when everything else was a little less stable.

There was a captain in my unit who was a part of a gang unit at the Metropolitan Police. If he ever met someone in trouble, he would steer them towards cadets and to our unit specifically. You know, the 'one last chance to turn your life around'. So we used to get a lot of people in our unit who were making some bad choices. Proper bad boys. And cadets did change quite a few of their lives for the better.

People say if you come from a broken home, it determines or sets up your future. But I disagree, because you can come from one-parent families, but if you've got a support system in place, like the cadets or an organisation that provides positive role models, you can still succeed. I think that, in this day and age, without that structure, without the right environment, without reminders and reassurances to stay on the right path, it is very easy to get into trouble. Cadets provided that for me. We were told repeatedly what was right and what was wrong. There was no space for confusion. If you did something wrong, you were punished for it. And because we were a unit, a team, any failure was shared. It wasn't just me letting myself down, it was me letting all of the cadets down. We were a team striving for the same goals, so I knew if I succeeded, we would all succeed.

Cadets set me up for life. I eventually got a very good education at Tenison's and managed to stay out of trouble. I did well in my exams and got a place at St Francis Xavier sixth form (or SFX), where the business side of me really came out. I was voted onto the student council and eventually became vice president, organising all of our events. We put on a lot of shows, at places like the Colosseum in Vauxhall. We even managed to get So Solid Crew to perform at one of our college dances. This was at the height of their fame. After I left SFX, I went to Kingston University to study Business and Information Technology.

I got a job at Barclays and was pursuing a few personal business projects on the side. Eventually I was introduced to somebody at RBS and from there went into corporate banking. I'm still in the corporate world, but now I deal primarily with governments and NGOs to try and deliver projects in Africa and other parts of the world.

*

I can hear you already. 'We know all this, Jeremiah. We want to help. But where can we start?' Excellent question! I thought I might begin by looking at some of the organisations that had the biggest impact on me when I was younger. I got my first experience of charity work through my mother, but from as far back as I can remember I somehow got involved with a number of initiatives. I was originally thinking of listing them at the back of the book, but it wouldn't really do them justice; they really belong in a full chapter about charity. I'm not recommending you go out and get involved with them all, but they are worth looking up at least, to give you a sense of the best way you can start giving back. Charity begins at home, in more ways than one.

One of the grassroots youth organisations I first got to know was the Triangle Adventure Playground in Oval, whose back fence separated it from my secondary school, Archbishop Tenison's. I first started going when I was very small, with my mum. It's a wonderful space, right in the heart of London, and one of the oldest children's charities in the area. This was a space that was another home away from home for me, when I was little. When I was very young, I would play with my brother and sister, giving my mum a well-earned break. When I became a little older, I would go with my friends after school finished, spending summer afternoons in the garden, or learning an activity in the centre.

Despite not being the biggest site, the Triangle is a solid part of the community, providing free lunches and activities in the holidays and looking after dozens of young people after school. Free spaces like these are essential for young people from low socio-economic backgrounds who live on the local housing estates. It not only allows them a place to grow and experiment and be themselves, it also provides much-needed help for working parents who are unable to afford childcare after school or in the holidays. Activities range from group sports games and gardening to indoor arts and crafts and DJ workshops. They also help to develop different life skills with activities such as cookery classes (just like my mum's), bicycle maintenance workshops and music lessons. The manager Jon is always a welcoming face, even when I run into him years after going to the playground.

The Triangle provides an essential service to the community and has helped generations of young people. However, it has had to fight for many years to stay open, partly due to their location on a prime piece of London real estate. Like many other youth projects, they had their funding cut a few years ago, but thankfully are still open and still going strong.

Fast-forward a few years, and I was beginning to pay attention to the work being done by charities to help young people get back on the right track. Juvenis is a charity that believes every young person deserves another chance. Headed by Winston Goode, Juvenis works to support the most vulnerable young people, especially those at risk of being arrested for being involved in crime. Through engagement in positive activities and one-on-one support, Juvenis keeps young people on the right path by providing advice, support and practical to help them get back into education or into training, employment or volunteering.

I first got to know Juvenis through one of their services, Divert Youth, an intervention programme to prevent young people in the criminal justice system from re-offending. Their team, with Lambeth Council, go and sit down with these young people while they're in police custody and just talk to them. As simple as it sounds, this act is the first time that many of these youths have been asked about themselves and how they're doing. This is used as a teachable moment to stop young people becoming first-time entrants into the criminal justice system. Together with the young people and their families, an action plan is created that includes: reintegrating them back into mainstream education, training or an apprenticeship; being assigned a mentor; and enrolment in an extra-curricular activity to divert them from a life of crime. As discussed in the education chapter, it's clear that interventions where young people are actively engaged and their well-being prioritised are necessary to prevent them from spiralling down a dark path.

There are other local groups taking a more direct approach to helping young people, focusing on the injustice and inequality that can be a root cause of crime. Recently, I saw an ICFree campaign in the middle of Brixton. ICFree are a group of advocates from the Advocacy Academy, a Social Justice Youth Organising Movement in Brixton. Young people who apply to the programme get to put together campaigns on things that they are passionate about. In this case, ICFree put up posters at bus stops around Brixton that highlighted how the Met Police disproportionally police young people of colour. One poster stated that more than half of children in prison are people of colour. These bold posters were then followed up with a protest in Brixton against the racism in schooling and policing. They highlighted the similarities between the internal exclusion (isolation) and expelling of young people of colour from school and the prison system, reiterating how keeping them in a silent room where they aren't learning doesn't rehabilitate them at all.

This campaign impressed me because ICFree were saying all the things that I and other young people had realised growing up, but didn't have the knowledge or vocabulary to speak out against. ICFree weren't just talking about it among themselves; they were going out on the streets to make sure that other people learned about this too. The Advocacy Academy, which ICFree grew out of, is the first organisation of its kind in the UK, and every year they help to empower a new group of young people to fight against the issues affecting them and their peers. What stands out for me is that this isn't about doing a one-off campaign and moving on; it's about teaching young people how to be advocates for life and continually fight against injustice. Their intention is they will not just inherit this mess, they will do something to fix it.

Spiral Skills is another organisation that I'd like to mention. Spiral Skills work with young people in schools and colleges to help them with their education and equip them with the skills and knowledge they need to succeed in the future. They work with young people who are doing their GCSEs but who are at risk of being expelled. Their interventions are designed around the fact that traditional methods of learning don't work for everyone. They deliver interactive workshops that focus on the career interests of the young people in the group and get them excited about their future. I got to know them through Karl Lokko, whom you met in the business chapter. Karl went to one of their sessions at a secondary school in Brixton and spoke to a class of young people about making positive decisions and holding themselves in higher esteem. This dedication to students who would usually be failed by the school system – in Karl's session a group made entirely of young black people – is what makes their work so necessary. As Damani stated previously, if there had been somebody to keep him in check or talk to him about how his future might turn out, he may have had an entirely different educational experience.

I can't finish this section without showing some love for the Hebe Foundation, which helped me to learn some skills so that I could found businesses and support young people. Hebe is a small organisation based in Clapham. They put me together with a group of other young people to create business plans based on what specifications real businesses needed, and then pitch the plan to them. The scheme was named 'Junior Apprentice', after the TV show. When we were successful we would be supported to bring some of our ideas to life, or we would do work experience sessions at the company we'd pitched to. There are a lot of reasons this one sticks out in my mind. Their support helped me make amazing friends and learn some of the qualities required for entrepreneurship. In fact, my most notable memory is when we walked into the Northern Trust investment bank for one of the challenges and didn't have any proper plan for our pitch, so I blagged the whole thing . . . and we ended up winning, funnily enough! However, more important than that, the reason Hebe is so dear to me now is because of the connections I made there. The team that worked with me became lifelong friends who support me to this day and I have the pleasure, every once in a while, of going back to help the young people who they are supporting now, all these years later.

Finally, as you might have guessed from Captain Acquah's testimony, there's the Army Cadets. I was an Army Cadet for most of my teenage life. In brief, the Army Cadets is a national youth group sponsored by the Ministry of Defence (MOD) and the British Army. There's no actual fighting, you'll be pleased to hear, but it's a great way to learn about military life and pick up some vital skills and connections along the way. I took part in a range of subjects from the Army Proficiency Certificate syllabus: navigation (with a map and compass), fieldcraft (learning about the outdoors, setting up harbour areas), shooting (marksmanship principles and how to control a rifle), first aid and more.

There's one other important aspect of the Army Cadets that stood out for me. It was the fact that all of the adults who were involved – looked after us and taught us – were volunteers. They took their own time out to help all of us young people. They came from a range of professions. The commanding officer of my sector, Colonel Ettingshausen, worked for the MOD and ran his own PR agency. Lieutenant Bambury worked in the events and hospitality sector. Captain Acquah was my unit commander, he was in the banking industry. All of these individuals had busy lives and each had a massive impact on me as a person. I've only mentioned three names here but, throughout my early life, I was fortunate to meet a number of talented, intelligent, dedicated and helpful volunteers. I wanted to find out why, with all of their commitments, they still found time to volunteer.

*

Sometimes you can seek causes out and sometimes a cause will find you. In 2013, I went to a party that would change my life for ever.

Young Black and Talented was an empowerment project delivered in the Brixton Road Youth Centre. It consisted of weekly meet-ups, outreach events and small-scale projects, all designed to help empower and uplift young women in the area. A lot of my female friends from school went and they often spoke about how inspiring and helpful the sessions were. One afternoon they invited me and some of my friends along to see what was going on. Looking back, I'm not sure why we thought they should (or would) let us boys attend, but luckily for us they did. This was at a time when we didn't really have anywhere else to go after school (apart from Bricky McDs) and I knew that, for a lot of the girls, the project was a lifeline.

As soon as we arrived, we were roped into helping to organise a Valentine's Day party they were planning, deliberating over the music and PA system, the lighting, the food, the special guests. We even wrote a song and planned to perform it in front of everyone. Everyone in the ends was invited to the party. A lot of the girls there were from our year in school, so at first we thought it should really only be for young people of our age, but then there was a group of older youths we thought should be there – a few older boys and girls we were friendly with, older brothers and sisters of our group, people we wanted to bring in. One of the key members of that group was a boy named Patrick, who had helped me a lot over the years. After I had been threatened on Facebook, he went out of his way to make me feel safe, walking me back through Brixton most afternoons. Patrick was also someone who got me into a lot of local youth groups and initiatives. We felt that, if anyone deserved to be at the party and get something back, it was Patrick.

The night of the party came and I was feeling nervous. I'd sung in a choir, but I'd never performed in public before, especially not in front of all of my friends. I was also regretting the subject matter of our song. It was all about first love. What was I thinking? Eventually, our time came and we got up on stage and looked around. The whole hall was packed. The beat started and we performed the song as best we could. We got a few claps, but I could see most of our friends laughing away.

I didn't mind though. I was having fun by this point. We carried on playing and partied for several hours, so I missed my curfew. Even though it was a bit raucous and noisy, the adults let us enjoy ourselves, kept a close eye on us and made sure everyone was OK.

I left the event with a girl I had a bit of a crush on. I walked her to the bus stop near her home, where we stood around chatting until my bus arrived. I gave her a big hug and jumped on, immediately spotting a familiar face in the back row. My mum! I quickly looked at the ground and shuffled my way upstairs, expecting the shouting to start at any minute . . . But it never came. I collapsed into a seat on the top deck. It was the closest miss ever, as I don't know what she would have done if she had seen me at the bus stop with a girl after my curfew. Mum, if you're reading this, I'm sorry!

Given everything that had happened, I hadn't really paid attention to who was at the party and who wasn't. The following day when I woke up, I remember feeling exhausted from the night before. I was thinking about rolling over and going back to sleep, but for some reason picked up my phone. I had a heap of missed calls and messages. My best friend Whiltz had sent me fifteen ping alerts on Blackberry Messenger. I knew something was wrong. The first message I opened simply said, 'RIP Patrick.' I immediately called Whiltz and he told me that Patrick had lost his life in the early hours of the morning. He hadn't come to the Valentine's Day party after all. He had gone to a friend's birthday party at a house in Brixton instead. There had been a fight and he had been stabbed trying to protect his friends.

I was shaken. My immediate thought was, Why? It made no sense. Patrick was a good guy, someone who always helped others. How could this happen to him? I got together with some of my closest friends. Everyone was shaken. Violence was an accepted part of all our lives, but this was something we couldn't understand. The murder was featured on the BBC news that evening, Patrick's smiling face beamed into homes across the country. It was too much for me.

With my friends and other young people we knew who were friendly with Patrick, we began to organise an event in Patrick's memory. It began as a single activity, but soon grew to become a day of events, all aimed at helping young people to thrive. We had a vision of taking over a space in central London, bringing in special guest speakers and securing funding to make it an annual event. We even gave it a name: Youth Empowerment Day. This was us doing something about the situation we found ourselves in. This was us not sitting by, waiting for another tragedy to happen. This was us trying to give back. But it was not to be.

*

Due to a lack of funding, Youth Empowerment Day sadly never happened. After the initial outpouring of grief and outrage, the support gradually fell away. But it gave me the idea for another project. I wanted to create an organisation to help reduce the amount of youth crime in the capital. I wanted to involve young people in the decision-making processes aimed at reducing crime and violence in their communities. I wanted to create a network of smaller groups to more effectively help young people put on events, share information and receive updates on key local decisions. I wanted to put the power back in young people's hands. A few months after Patrick's death, I officially launched One Big Community.

We initially held a number of events to raise awareness about the issue of knife crime and youth violence in the capital. We started with One Big Debate, an online debate on Twitter that was driven by young people. We trended number one in the UK as we discussed various different ideas to tackle youth violence. All of a sudden, something which had existed only in my head had become a reality. And what's more, the conversations were moving towards real change. People were moving beyond general problems and causes to consider what they could do now, in their area. I was so happy. Out of the grief of Patrick's death something good was emerging.

We held various other events, residential activities and even a debate at City Hall in London. We called it the Wall of Silence; an opportunity for young people to speak directly to a panel of decision-makers from the world of politics, the media, business and healthcare. We felt that opportunities for people in power to hear directly from the people whose lives their decisions were affecting were few and far between. We recognised a wall of silence between the panellists and the young people. This event was a chance to break that silence. Soon after, we were invited to host the Youth Justice Convention, which led to a few of us addressing the prime minister and MPs directly in the Houses of Parliament.

In the time following Patrick's death, youth activism had become my world. It is a feeling like no other to create a platform for young people's voices to be heard, while also helping the people in power to see the reality behind the news headlines. I saw how much we were able to do with so little, and began to picture what might be possible if we could scale up the organisation significantly. But I was also frustrated. We were being heard, on the biggest stages possible, but little was actually being done. I was being invited to the same events, the same panels, the same discussions, but there was minimal action from the government or local authorities. We were still being targeted by the police. Youth services were still nonexistent. No meaningful investment was being made in the communities that needed it the most. I was fifteen at this point but, as passionate and dedicated as I was, I was also exhausted. There was little room in my life for anything else and I knew I either had to take a step up and see what else could be done, or take a step back and finish school.

I moved on from One Big Community just before I turned sixteen. It was an incredible journey, from start to finish. I had seen young people come together to change public policy, to bring together communities, to try and save lives and so much more. I found a way to address some of the most important issues facing young people today, using young people – people with burning desires and comprehensive skills – to make meaningful change. For all the frustration, I had learned a valuable lesson. I had the power to influence change. It was our time to be heard.

*

Victor

Eventually I re-joined the cadets and became a captain myself. It was a simple decision. I wanted to give back.

I think people of colour in the UK have a particularly hard time. I'm not just talking about black people.

Institutional racism is real. So in order to succeed we need to help each other. If we don't help each other, then maybe one person will succeed, but we really need whole communities to succeed. I used to have the mindset that you should only do something if you're getting properly compensated for it. It took a while for me to change that. What matters more is the good you're putting out into the world.

The seed that was planted grew. I thought I could offer something back. You know, I remembered that there were people at the community centres when I was growing up who were knowledgeable. You had the IT gurus, you had the people who could help with university applications, you had people who worked in social services who knew what to do in certain situations. You had people you knew you could speak to who, for the most part, would offer good advice and not judge or belittle you. I know I'm banging on about this a bit, but you really can't place a value on that for young people growing up in difficult circumstances. Instead of a trusted adult, children are finding that person in the wrong places. I knew a lot about the world of finance and I also wanted to help. I thought I could become that person who listens.

We never turn anyone away. If you try, you are in. We're an inclusive unit in the sense that, even if you are described as 'difficult' or 'troubled' in some way, we will always try to help you. At cadets, you are part of something much bigger, part of a family. We get that you may not be the cleverest person in the classroom. We get that you're not in the popular clique. But at cadets, you belong. You are always part of the family.

I mean, I have heard stories about domestic violence. I've heard stories about extreme poverty and homelessness. I've heard stories about drug abuse or young people being groomed by gangs, doing stuff that could get them a lengthy custodial sentence or even killed. I've seen kids with real anger issues as a result of what's going on at home. People don't really see that. Teachers don't see that. Politicians don't see that. I'm not a social worker. It's not really my job to help a family get back on its feet. Sometimes they don't want it. I've tried to help before and it's backfired. But through my work with the cadets, I can really help young people.

The issues the young people I work with face are a lot worse today than when I was growing up. There are a lot more gang issues, especially in London, and there's a lot more violence. I know I'm going to sound old now, but back in the day, we used to sort things out with our fists. Maybe someone would know someone with a gun, but it was not as common as it is today. Now, everybody has knives. That's the minimum, you know. A lot more people have access to guns, handguns and some people even have access to automatic rifles. And these crimes are messages. 'Leave my crew alone or this is going to happen to you.' That's why some of these stabbings and shootings are so gruesome and so awful. Some of these gangs are making serious money. I've seen boys with £50,000 chains, £20,000 watches. Driving expensive cars, posting about their riches on social media. You can't do that without having the armoury to back it up. Gone are the days when you could have a moped and be the top boy of the block.

I care because I've seen the effects of drugs, I've seen the effects of gangs, I've seen the effects of violence. I've seen good people who I went to school with turn out to be drug addicts, begging on the streets, losing their minds. Mental illness is something that is prevalent in our society, but we don't talk about it that much, you know? So I've seen a lot of good people who I've laughed with and kicked a football about with go the wrong way. And because they've gone the wrong way, their kids are now on a bad path. We know that if the streets haven't got them already, the drug dealers and other bad influences, then maybe we can get in there first and influence them to follow the right path. We're trying to suck you into our system, before you can get sucked into the other one.

There have even been occasions when some of the kids have gone back to gangs and we've had to pull them out. Some of the kids we work with have real anger issues. For them, it's a point of principle to disobey orders. I know some of the gang leaders and think they have a little bit of *respect for me, so I've been able, once or twice, to pull someone back. You see some people arrive and you think, 'Oh my gosh, is this person going to survive?' But then ten years later they're settled, they have children, they're in a good job and you know deep down that it's the cadets that have put them on the right path.*

*

My first ever proper job was as a youth consultant at Big Change. Big Change is a charitable organisation that exists to 'reimagine education', by no means a small goal. Their conversations and research revolve around what education really means, what it should mean, and what support organisations need to make the real changes that will transform the lives of young people across the UK. I first got involved with them when I was just sixteen on their 'growth mindset' research and campaign. The Big Change team was looking at how having the right mindset can drastically change how we learn. One of the most important things in this book for me is the exploration I make of the paradigms through which people look at the world, and how this affects their actions. The growth mindset research we explored is a fundamental part of under-standing that. Instead of viewing events and failures as the full extent of what we can achieve and letting that define us (which is known as a fixed mindset), Big

Change thoroughly explored a vastly superior para-digm: the growth mindset. In contrast to thinking that you can't change your situation, with a growth mind-set, you believe that you always have the room to learn, change and improve your skills and abilities. With a true growth mindset, you don't just accept that things are the way they are; instead, you challenge them and use any failures as an opportunity to grow. You might seek feedback, take time to reflect or seek new oppor-tunities at every turn; these are all characteristics of someone with a strong growth mindset.

I would say that this mentality is true of young people today or, at least, of a lot of the young people I have been able to support and interact with. However, this piece of research only came about because we felt that too many young people didn't believe in themselves, or thought they couldn't change the situations they were born into, and that the education system should be helping to resolve that. This idea is the foundation for much of the work I've done in the years since, to inspire young people and work with organisations which sup-port and uplift those who might be left behind.

I was so inspired by Big change's mission that I helped them to establish their Youth Advisory Board and con-tinued working with them behind the scenes to ensure their work reached as many young people as possible. At the age of sixteen, myself and eleven other young people representing several organisations came together in the Virgin head offices in London, where Big Change are based, to learn about their work, contribute to it, scrutinise it, and take all of that back to our communities.

My main takeaway from my time with Big Change, other than understanding education more holistically and what a growth mindset is (two sizeable things in themselves), is the togetherness and energy that is facilitated by a strong youth board. This is the main reason I love setting them up for other organisations – because the potential impact on the institution and on the lives of those young people is absolutely mind-blowing. It's that energy that I want to see and inspire more of, because I truly believe that the way to encourage more cohesive and diverse work is by bringing people together in such a way, to break down barriers and contribute to organisations that are already having a meaningful impact. Finally, one of the people I met on the Big Change youth board was Seven Jacobs, now a close friend and business partner of mine. At the time, we were just young people on a youth board together, but over time we began working together more closely. That's made a great impact on me.

So what has working with all these different groups shown me? One thing is that a huge amount of power for change can be generated in a very short amount of time if young people are allowed to mix socially and be socially mobile, because that is when the explosion of ideas and energy is at its peak – when diversity is allowed to flourish. I've also had my eyes opened wide to the strength that young people have to change the world through activism. With the right mindset, one in which your situation is not fixed and you can improve, and the right environment – where different people with different ideas and experiences can come together to get good work done – the potential goes beyond changing just local communities. It creates a real will to influence policies, views, institutions and governments, as well as family, friends and schools. Therefore, it is the power to change the world for the better.

*

Victor

I think volunteering should be compulsory. Imagine what society would be like if everyone gave a bit of their free time to help others. Imagine the skills and experience young people could access and make use of. I strongly believe that, as much as you take from society, you need to give back. I would be lost if it wasn't for the cadets, so I see it as my duty and my privilege to help other young people. Social responsibility should be taught in schools.

What I've seen emerge in all of the cadets we've worked with is leadership. It's strength. It's the confidence to act on your beliefs and do the right thing. It's a can-do attitude. I've been so impressed with so many of the young people we've worked with – young people who, when they joined, couldn't look us in the eye, and then a year or two later they are delivering presentations in front of 200 people, making people laugh, helping the younger cadets, showing care and compassion, leading by example. It's a wonderful thing. This is a cliché, but they are people of integrity. The cadets didn't create that integrity, they just helped to bring it forwards. These are young people you can trust. Young people you know won't let you down.

We are helping at the source. This is not just cadets I'm talking about now, this is youth projects and volunteers who work with young people in general. If we can ease the pressure of struggling families, that's a good thing. If we can help young people to become decent citizens, then that's a good thing. That work is repaid. Those young people can inspire others. It's about developing people so they can get to a position where they can make a positive difference to their community.

It's about giving back. You cannot succeed on your own. Somebody was there for you in order for you to get to where you are. I think it's important to realise that you didn't get there by yourself. Humility is important. When you volunteer, you get a satisfaction or a certain gratification from it because you can see the difference you've made. You've helped somebody get from A to B. That's better than any pay cheque. There's a joy in seeing someone who had come into cadets as a shy person transform and leave sure of themselves. Bumping into this confident person later in life and finding out they're thriving when they could have gone sideways, that fills me with happiness.

For me personally, I feel like this is the way to get to young people. And if you can do a good job with one young person, then it can only benefit the community because there's the school of thought that they will tell somebody else and that person will tell somebody else and then it grows organically. You know, word of mouth is a very powerful communication tool.

Across the UK, we're seeing the poor getting poorer and the rich getting richer. The social divide is starker now that it's ever been, I believe. And I can't see it getting any better. I'm not going to pretend that I have the solutions either. The cadets aren't going to pull someone out of poverty or stand in for what's really missing in young people's lives. But what they can offer is an opportunity.

*

So, why did I spend so many pages just describing youth organisations that I care about? It comes down to the pieces of learning that I took from every single one of them and how they contributed to my understanding the potential of youth activism. I see my teenage years as a puzzle where, with each significant new experience and organisation, I discovered a new piece that I could use to complete the bigger picture.

Having a growth mindset; re-imagining education; social mobility; enterprising experience; equal opportunity; community development. These are the ideas that stick out in my mind when I think about change. Here is how each one of them contributes to a recipe for successful change:

Growth mindset: If you as an individual decide that, no matter your circumstances, current skills or past events, you are going to make a difference, then you will. If you have a fixed mindset instead and believe that you can't change anything, then you won't – because you'll never work to make it happen. Easier said than done, I realise, but a simple shift in attitude can make the world of difference.

Education: Too often, we confuse what education is for what our education system looks like, which at the moment doesn't work for everyone. Instead, we should be thinking about constantly educating ourselves and those around us and contributing to expanding opportunities to learn beyond the academic world of school and homework. In this way, what we learn in and out of school will be the things that we need to 'thrive in life, not just in exams', as Big Change would put it.

Social mobility: If the last two qualities were things you can do within yourself or decisions you can make about your own life, then this is about taking that outside of yourself and bringing different people together who want to put their unique qualities to good use. Instead of seeing differences as things that divide us, view them as opportunities to learn something new or to develop skills from, which you can then mix into your own work and personal life. At the end of the day, there is nothing more similar to one human being than another; we will always have more in common than not, but we can learn from the differences that do exist, gaining new skills and perspectives, which we can carry into every piece of work we do and every relationship we create and foster.

Enterprise: Young people in today's modern world are naturally very enterprising, utilising creativity, innovative ideas and collaboration to create solutions, rather than just talking about problems. This is what I believe will fundamentally allow us to actually make the changes that our activism promotes.

Equal opportunity: As history has shown us, it is a real and ongoing struggle to overcome the divisions and inequalities around us. But we can push to make this happen, by banding together to get the hard work done and, through our everyday decisions, to advocate for others. Include other people, get them involved, ask them their opinions and work to make sure everyone is treated fairly. Your activism could include people of all backgrounds to make sure of this, or it could highlight injustices that particular groups face. But getting diverse people from all sections of society together is what will make that change happen, so ensure that everyone gets the opportunity to participate and contribute. Perhaps you could even bring totally different communities together to make something happen!

Community development: Bringing together people who unite over certain issues enables them to show their collective passion for a cause – and without passion, nothing will be achieved. Connect your communities – local, school, online or otherwise – so that everyone is prepared to make change together. Then you can expand your movement from there! For example, the climate change movements that have exploded over the last year of writing this book, which have been led through online communities, have been able to harness the support of the global community in a very short time! Just think outside the box about how you can get this done.

So, to every young person reading this, I want you to understand one thing. I'm not going to tell you to go build or find these qualities, because you need to do what is right for you in your own life. I would, however, encourage you to understand them and the potential they have to change your life and the lives of those around you, because the feeling that comes from successfully changing to incorporate them is incredible. And, to everyone reading this who has young people in their lives, no matter who they are or what community they are a part of, I want you to find ways of bringing these qualities into their lives to help them reach their goals and achieve their dreams. And, of course, there is also nothing stopping you from adopting these qualities yourself.

Conclusion

I've been dreaming in a nightmare
Living here you might fear
Reminiscing on my life
Giving thanks I'm still alive
You could be the calmest person
But still get some enemies
Friends taken away from me
All my brothers rest in peace
Fire in my heart
Heart burns and understatement
If dreaming is illegal
You can take me to the station.

*

There was a period in my life where I couldn't see the future. I didn't believe I would live to see my twentieth birthday. I grew up in a place filled with uncertainty and fear, and I was uncertain and fearful for many years. I grew up in a place where your best friend could vanish overnight, or a fellow student could get a life sentence. I grew up in a place where I wasn't listened to. I grew up in a place where I was expected to fail. I am not talking about south London, here. I need to be clear about something: I am in no way suggesting that my area, or areas like the one I grew up in, are nightmares. The nightmare is not a physical place. In some ways, however, that place has only had a positive effect on my life. It has given me motivation, and ambition, and community. It's given me reserves of energy and strength I never knew I had. Writing this book has been one of the most difficult things I have ever done. However, it's made me realise how far I've come. Sometimes you forget along the way.

When I was sixteen, nearly seventeen, a few bad things happened to me. It all began with the charity I had helped to set up. It was a success. We were fulfilling our promises to help young people, and we were recognised for it. I was spending a lot of my spare time working at the charity, speaking at events, or meeting decision-makers and local leaders to see what else we could do. Everything was going well, until it wasn't. I discovered that the charity wasn't doing everything that it was supposed to be doing. We had set up a system to enable the charity to work effectively, but it wasn't operating correctly. I was being used, but I was also being pushed away. There wasn't very much that I could do. I was sixteen, after all. We tried to fight, but in the end, the stress of it all was too much. I had to step away. It felt like I could at least return to my schoolwork, focus on my exams, make sure I gave myself the best possible start to my working life. And then my mother fell ill.

My mum has always struggled with health issues. It got so bad when we were very young that we had to go into care for a little bit while she recovered. At that time she was going through a difficult period. She was in bed with a bad case of the flu, but isn't wasn't getting any better. I was in college one day and got a call from my brother, who said that she was having difficulty breathing, and that he was going to call an ambulance. I got back at around the same time as the ambulance arrived. We knew something serious was wrong from the way they were behaving. They measured mum's heartrate and said the she was tachycardic, which meant that she was at risk of a heart attack, and rushed her off to hospital, blue lights flashing.

She was placed in the resuscitation room. That was one of the scariest moments in my life. We were surrounded by people who were seriously ill. Someone had just been airlifted in from a road traffic accident, someone had been stabbed. My mum was talking but we had no idea what might happen. It was a big moment for me and my brother and sister. We were still teenagers but we had to grow up. We realised that we had to look after my mum now. We didn't have a dad or someone else to look to.

Mum had pneumonia and heart failure, and was in and out of hospital for the next few weeks. It was really on us to look after ourselves. My mum was our world. There were times when I was growing up when I was angry at her for our situation, but she has always been there for us. She has given up so much just to make sure that we had something. She has always been the rock each of our lives is based on.

A week and a half after my mum was discharged, I was out with a friend in Brixton. I had given a talk at a university the evening before, and had a bit of money from that, so we went to JD Sports to buy some new trainers. We came out of the shop and cut through the market when we saw a group of boys sprinting off in different directions. A couple of them came towards us, chased by a gang of shopkeepers, men with wooden planks and pipes and whatnot. They caught them and grabbed them – pushing them and shouting. One of the boys was a friend from school, so we ran over to see what was going on. It turns out that the friend had been with another group who had stolen a phone from a shop round the corner and run off. We tried to calm the situation, telling the men to wait for the police, but they didn't listen, and started attacking our friend and the boy he was with. Then from out of nowhere I was punched in the face, and my friend was dragged onto the ground. I grabbed the man who had punched me, still shouting about the police, and could see my friend in the middle of a circle of men getting kicked and punched, hit with metal bars and planks of wood, blood all over his face. I let go of the man I was holding and dived on top of my friend, trying to pull him away. I could feel blows landing on my body. Something hit me in my eye and all of a sudden I couldn't see. I began shuffling backwards pulling my friend and eventually the blows stopped, and the circle dispersed. I could hear sirens.

I later found out that I had been punched with a knuckle-duster. My eye was completely shut and I had a nasty cut underneath my eyebrow. The metal had missed my eyeball by about half a centimetre. Me and my friend were covered in bruises, our clothes torn and dirty. All of this over nothing. A young black boy had taken something from a shop and so the shopkeepers and market traders had targeted whichever black boy they could find. This wasn't a citizen's arrest, this was vigilante justice.

Eventually the police turned up, and everyone scattered. I was just about standing up, clutching my friend, holding my face. Blood was dripping between my fingers and onto the ground. The police sat us down in the boot of a police car and called an ambulance. I just remember pleading with them not to call my mum, but they did. I felt so ashamed. I knew that the last thing she needed was more stress, and now her youngest son was on his way to hospital. I thought she would be disappointed in me.

I got home, but for some reason the attack stayed with me. I couldn't shake it. My schoolwork was suffering. I was missing days, then weeks. Teachers noticed, and I started seeing a counsellor. I was as low as I have ever been. In the end I felt as though the only thing I could do was to remove myself from everyone and everything. I stopped going to school altogether and stayed at home. It didn't feel like I was living a nightmare. I just didn't want to dream anymore.

*

I recognise that this book tells only a few stories. It's about my life, primarily, so it's a very subjective and one-sided account. What I'm trying to do here, however, is use my life (short as it's been) to shine a spotlight onto the experiences of a lot of young people in London, and across the UK, in an attempt to help everyone better understand some of the key issues of today, and the truth behind the headlines.

That's all very nice, I hear you say. But what good will it do? Will it really make a difference? Probably not. But I hope it will prompt readers who are younger and older to ask a few more questions, at least.

Let's go back to the beginning. Identity for me was the only possible place to start this book. It's a question that I think a lot of people don't really consider enough, and one that really does have profound implications for how people see themselves, and are seen. I'm proud of my heritage, and I'm glad I've had an opportunity to explore more of my past, and my family's past in the writing of this book. Nigeria will always be home for me, in some sense, even though I've never been. But I'm also connected to Britain. I may not always feel like I belong, but I was born here. The important point to make is that only you know who you are. Don't let anybody make that decision for you, and don't let your identity hold you back.

Home is something I have spent a lot of time searching for, and something a lot of people take for granted. The number of young people living in temporary or inadequate accommodation is high, and rising. I live in Croydon now, and south London will always be my home, but it's taken me years to feel a sense of security, to feel rooted.

In my area, a lot of bad things happen, so young people often feel they need to carry a knife for protection. They've got no one to tell them otherwise. I'm lucky. I've been surrounded by positive things my entire life, and even I have felt at times that carrying a knife might be a good idea, even though I have never done it. Now imagine you grow up without that level of positivity. What options do you have? Youth violence has a number of causes, and is, more often than not, the result of a lack of opportunities, poor education and domestic violence or difficulties at home. It's caused by cuts in public funding over a number of years. It's caused by a failing welfare state. It's caused by a school system that prefers to exclude its most needy pupils instead of helping them. In spite of what the newspapers say, it's not a problem that is limited to a particular race. It does, however, point to a much broader break in society.

I could keep going. I don't need to spell out the benefits of charity, or the importance of change, or why children need to be given more of a chance in schools. What I'd like to focus on here are a few general rules that have helped me, and that I hope can help you too.

Be brave. You *can* change your immediate surroundings. You can change your world. All you have to do is take a jump. The resounding message that can be found within the book is grabbing opportunities. As discussed, I didn't have many in front of me, but whenever I did, I tried to take the jump. Change is a word, but we need it to become an action. This is something that I finish most of my talks by saying this. We all seek change, whether that's in our personal lives, business, family, it's a constant process. But how can we expect any change to come if we do not take the necessary action to making it happen. Have you got a business idea? Have you got an issue you're passionate about tackling? DO you want to get involved in something special but don't know how to? The easiest first step is plotting your idea down on paper. Visualising is very important, and without it we can find ourselves living a life full of uncertainty.

Look ahead. I try to talk to my future self. There is no surer way to gain a fresh perspective on any thorny problem than to speak to yourself in 20 years. Your future self is very wise. They know what will bring you peace, ease, and joy. As Bill Gates admits, most of us at 40, 60, even 80, remain in a dialogue with our 20-year-old. This is not a life-affirming dialogue, because at 50, your 20-year-old self thinks you are old and past it. Your 70-year-old self, on the other hand, will tell your 50-year-old person, correctly, that you will never be so young, powerful, vital or fit again. Yourself in 20 years is wise. They know not to sweat the small stuff. They know what will bring you joy. When you have 15 quiet minutes alone, do this easy future-self visualization. A word of advice: If you are at an age where you do not feel, realistically, that you will be alive in 20 years from now, but still want to access a wisdom that eludes you, try imagining speaking to yourself from beyond the grave. What would your long-dead self tell you to do or say right now?

Follow through on your commitments. Nothing gives you a greater sense of your power than when you do what you've said you'll do. Empowerment coaches call this 'manifesting.'

None of us are in control of every outcome, but we can each be absolutely in control of doing what we've said we'll do. And this makes us feel powerfully alive. It draws others towards us. To be your word, it may mean reducing what you commit to, but if you do not follow through on commitments, not only will others stop trusting you, but you will stop believing in yourself. And how joyful is a life where you can't count on yourself?

Believe in yourself. When I want something, I get it. I will remove all doubt. I refuse to allow failure to be an option. If I apply for a grant, or for a position, I don't sit around waiting and wondering what might happen. I'm impatient for the confirmation that I have succeeded.

Be thankful. Dreaming in a nightmare is a concept that anyone can relate to. You may find that there is an aspect of your life, your day to day reality, that can be seen as a nightmare to someone else. One day I was at a restaurant London, having a catch up with two friends from Kenya. They are a successful couple who have built a number of different businesses across different industries. We were discussing this concept. They told me about one night a few months before that moment, they held a dinner at their home with a friend. They began speaking about family. He told them about his wife and kids and some of the financial struggles he was experiencing. He commented on their wealth and extravagant lifestyle. He said that they had everything, and he had close to nothing.

They turned around and told him how unhappy they were. They were not been able to have children. They mentioned how their wealth meant nothing to them. The joy of having children would complete their world. This is just one example. Not long after the dinner, I took a trip to West Africa with the to.org creative activist group. On the trip some of us went to visit a rubbish dump to see an up cycling charity programme in action. When we got to the dump I spotted a lady walking through the rubbish with a baby strapped to her back. She was sifting through the rubbish, picking up and collecting any items she thought could be reused. I couldn't believe it. To me, the scene was a nightmare. But for the woman, it was a means of making real money. Not much, but enough. She could provide for her children. Even though I was impacted by various different issues, and held back from many opportunities, I came to the realisation that my reality could be seen as a dream to someone else. A roof over my head, free healthcare, even just clean water. Dreaming in a nightmare isn't about your socio-economic background or race. It's about the fact that we're all human beings, and we all have our desires and aspirations. We all have dreams. We are all blessed in our own ways.

*

As I write this, just before the book goes to print, we are still on lockdown in the midst of the Covid-19 pandemic.

In late January 2020, my life and the lives of those around me changed for good. The emergence of a new virus that no one had encountered before threatened life as we know it. And within moments, our lives were different, for many turned upside down. It is too early to know what the future holds, but it is certain that the world we emerge into will be a very different place, in ways both big and small. My worry now is that the pandemic and its aftermath will widen divisions in society, between rich and poor, between young and old. The impact on working families, on those in precarious employment, on those in inadequate housing (or even housing without outside space), on workers helping to keep our cities running or tackling the virus on the frontline, is all too clear.

I am one of the lucky ones. Many of my business interests were bought to a halt, and the publication of this book had to be moved back. Like the rest of the country and most of the world, I was not allowed to come into physical contact with my family, or visit my mum, given her underlying health issues. I lost several people who were very close to me, including my godmother, who this book is dedicated to. But I'm healthy. I still have ideas. I try to take the positives out of what is an over-whelmingly negative situation.

And I noticed something else. The usual low-level buzz of violence and crime in my area died down. There was a rush of creativity, an emergence of hidden entrepreneurs, activists, artists and educators. More young people making their voices heard. Amongst the nightmare, there were still dreamers.

*

Let's go back to that dark period.

Me alone, in my room, a scar taking shape on my eyelid, day after day. And then one afternoon, a friend from school came round. He told me to get up. He gave me, for a few seconds at least, a bit of faith in myself again. So I did get up. I managed to go back to school. I returned to counselling, and it started to help. Step by step, I started to get my confidence back. I caught up on my schoolwork. I started to reengage with my charity projects. I got back into cadets. One Friday, after preparing for a first-aid competition, I went to a house party, and met Daryl. I had something to give him.

I'm not dreaming all the time, but now I know how to do it. If this book does anything, I hope it gives you something. I hope it gives you the courage to dream.

Epilogue

I use the phrase 'dreaming in a nightmare' to describe my life and journey to date. In the past, I have used it specifically when talking about the experiences of my peers and myself, but I now believe that almost all of us can relate to this very same phrase. As I write this, we are still in the midst of a global pandemic.

At the beginning of the pandemic, I was in a state of shock. I had not fathomed how drastic the changes to all of our lives would be. Almost overnight, my world became virtual; I was spending more time in the digital world than ever before. I would eagerly tune in to the news every morning, afternoon, and evening, checking to see if there were any updates. It felt like a never-ending news cycle, with the same information repeated 24/7. The increasing list of measures that were put in place to protect the population left me feeling restricted. For the first time in my life, I was confined to a space, and had a fear of leaving.

At the same time, however, I also felt a sense of relief; it was almost as if the nightmare I have described within the book was slowly disappearing. Crime levels fell, and my hometown was no longer a war zone. Having everyone indoors created an absence of trauma, both physically and emotionally. Many of the nightmares I have described no longer existed; I was not waiting anxiously every day for a distasteful update. It felt as though the pandemic had given way to a short-term resolution and, for once, it felt peaceful.

Slowly, the feeling of peace faded away, and a feeling of isolation crept in to take its place. I had dreamt of independence for most of my life, and when I turned twenty, I decided it was the perfect age to start to provide for myself, to make key decisions about my own future – without relying on the guidance of others. So I moved out of my family home and into a new place. Excited was an understatement. Then, boom. The first lockdown began. Suddenly, new restrictions were put in place and I was unable to see my family.

Although I had always craved independence, being away from home and unable to see anyone was completely out of the ordinary. I missed my family more than ever. My new address felt more like a place of residence than a home, especially without my mum and siblings around, and I felt incredibly alone. My mother, who was quite vulnerable due to illness, had to shield, and for the first time ever I was away from her for a prolonged period. My mother is my strength and being

away from her was my kryptonite. I would often ago-
nise about how close in distance my mum was, but
understood I could not make physical contact. With
the easing of restrictions, there came a sense of guilt
about seeing her. I understood that this virus, this
invisible thing, could cause sickness and death, and at
the time of writing this, I have not given my mum a hug
in over a year.

During this time, I came to value the meaning of family
more than ever. I felt I had taken some of my personal
relationships for granted. It was more important than
ever to check on loved ones and to remember that we
were all experiencing the same thing. I did feel a sense
of belonging, and togetherness, but not in a positive
way. There was a new killer in town. A killer that could
not be combated by law enforcement, a killer that not
many people understood. Death was a major theme
across social media, a major topic in conversations, and a
major thought for all of us. It felt as if, on a global level,
everyone was speaking a universal language. We were
all working towards the same goal of sorting out the
pandemic so that we could get out of this situation and
move on.

I remember in my early childhood discovering the class
divide in the UK. It was after taking the 345 bus route
for the first time, going from South to West London,
that I realised there were two different worlds, one of

which I had never seen or experienced before. Two communities, in one of the greatest cities in the world, so close but so far – the embodiment of social distancing. However, with coronavirus, people from both communities, wealthy and poor, could closely relate to each other. A whole nation locked down, trembled to the ground. All citizens cast away from loved ones and everyone experiencing the same nightmare.

Once the shock subsided, the first couple of weeks were the easiest. Everyone presumed that the lockdown would be a short-term solution, a quick interlude before life returned to normal; however, it was only the beginning. I spoke to my mum regularly, primarily to check that she was OK, but also because it was important to hear all the updates about her health. Like everyone, she was avoiding leaving the house and had reduced contact with her family. It was a tough moment when the reality kicked in that I would not be able to make physical contact with her, and now it is sadly just the new normal.

Before this pandemic, I had never valued the importance of a hug – a basic form of human contact. Although hard, it was reassuring to remember that millions of people were experiencing the same thing, some unable even to visit relatives in hospitals and care homes. It gave me perspective on the situation and allowed me to work through the emotion.

On top of feeling isolated, for the first time in my life I felt completely trapped and helpless. My future was filled with so much uncertainty. Up to this point, I thought I had understood my purpose. I am on this earth to give back and to change the community around me. But now, the question 'Who is Jeremiah?' was seemingly on repeat in my head. The pandemic had knocked my confidence; I felt I was back in a whirlwind of confusion. How could I give back if we were in crisis mode? What could I possibly do? Was I even good enough for myself? There were times when I thought I wanted to be ordinary again. I thought about stepping out from the spotlight and avoiding that scrutiny from others. I didn't want to be the person that other people relied on and I didn't want to be the one carrying out all of the work. The thoughts amplified, and I even took a few breaks from social media to try and cure these new feelings of angst.

Self-doubt crept up on me, and I felt like I had two options. I could take the easy way out and give it all up, or I could fight this feeling. It became clear that running away wasn't an option. I reminded myself that I had a task to do that was far from completed. I needed to work towards changing the world around me in the ways I had dreamt of over the years. I was determined; no virus was going to stop me.

On top of that, I had to think about how I could generate income. The obvious option was to put some more time into one of my hobbies. I had been passionate about music for a very long time, and decided it was time to focus on starting my independent record label and use it as a way to rediscover my purpose. Even though the music industry was being impacted by the pandemic, I knew I could still receive income from streaming and public performance. I decided to focus on building up my brand, and creating a strong team who could help turn the vision into a reality. As a multi-purpose entertainment company, Just Ents, we are developing the tools and resources to provide everything that an established or emerging artist might need to boost or kick-start their career. We cover an array of different areas, from management, distribution and publishing, to life coaching, financial consultancy and mental health support.

Through partnerships, we deliver group well-being sessions and one-to-one coaching support for artists and their management teams. The stress of becoming famous, sometimes overnight, can have a huge impact on artists' mental health, and therefore on their managers too. We want to enable them to live healthy and fulfilling lives and build meaningful careers that positively affect the lives of others.

I had found myself at an uncertain place. My consultancy business had been hit by the pandemic but I was determined to persevere. Although I was at my lowest point, I used it as an opportunity to identify something else I was interested in. It was not always easy, and there are three examples I want to share with you that helped me overcome the more challenging times.

1. Breathe

One Monday afternoon I was piled with work. I had so much to catch up on. We were on the verge of sealing a partnership between Just Ents and a major distributor. At the same time, one of the artists on our roster was going through some personal issues. I was also quite worried about the health of my mum, as she had mentioned the previous day she felt unwell. By 6 p.m. I felt defeated; I had so many tasks to get done, and it was only the start of the week.

I remembered an exercise I had learned from a colleague. Its purpose was to clear your mind, which often feels clouded during high-stress scenarios. I decided to try it. I sat down on my living room floor, closed my eyes and focused solely on my breathing. Over the duration of ten seconds, I took a breath in, followed by a ten-second count to release the breath out. I followed this exercise for sixty seconds. My mind was totally cleared and I felt uplifted, like the weight of the world had been lifted off my shoulders. Instead of being stressed out by everything, I came to realise the solution was to tackle each problem head on, one by one.

Can you remember the last time you sat in silence to breathe? This was something I had to learn to do. We often find ourselves prioritising being busy over being still, but taking time just to breathe has huge benefits.

2. Focus

It was 6 a.m. and the alarm on my phone woke me up. It was light outside and as I lay in bed, I could hear the trains passing outside my house. Instinctively, I picked up my phone, entered my passcode and immediately opened the Twitter app. I had four new direct messages and a few notifications from a tweet I had shared the night before. I went on to browse the other apps – Instagram, Snapchat, Gmail: the usual. When I raised my head to look at the time, two hours had passed and it was suddenly 8 a.m.

I had a moment of realisation then that my phone use was becoming excessive. Every day it was a repeated cycle: as soon as I opened my eyes I would turn to my phone. It is unhealthy, unproductive, and can cloud your mind before your day has even started.

For many people, this is part of our morning routine. I decided that I wanted to break this habit and I challenge everyone to do the same. At first it was hard, and I started by putting my phone in another room to avoid temptation. I also challenged myself to see the sun every morning before touching my phone, incorporating a walk into my daily routine. It took some time to get used to, but it has really improved my mornings.

3. Forward

In uncertain times, it can often feel like you have to live life day by day. I found myself stuck at a crossroads where I couldn't visualise the future. Planning seemed pointless with the world changing every day. At the beginning of 2020, I had the year mapped out. In the lead-up to the book release, my team and I had thought about many different marketing ideas and events that we wanted to put into action. I had planned interviews, collaborations and even competitions.

When the news of the pandemic hit, all my plans began to be cancelled one by one. I had a whole page of ideas I wanted to put together, and by May this was reduced to one sentence. This made me very anxious as the book's publication day approached. No one had ever released a book in these circumstances before; there were no case studies we could follow. There was one key lesson I learned during this time. I could think about all the problems for as long as I wanted to, but I needed to start thinking about solutions. I found a great way to do this was to plan on a weekly basis. Each Sunday I aimed to identify five key areas I wanted to work towards each week. With time, this became a great way to channel my energy for the week ahead and it felt easier to focus on the next seven days, rather than the rest of the year.

You may feel overwhelmed and disheartened, but I want to remind you that there are still things in your control. Try out the techniques that I've shared and, once you embrace them, you will be reminded that you have the power to make small changes in your everyday that will ultimately lead to bigger changes and a positive impact.

I too feel like the nightmare of Covid is continuous, maybe it is never-ending. However, for billions of us across the world, we now co-exist in a nightmare we could never have predicted. We've become more physically disconnected, and yet more virtually connected than we ever imagined. My question to answer is: how can we turn these times into a positive? And how can we all move ourselves forward in this new world that is holding us back?

Notes

Introduction

p.3   **'For a long time I'd been applying . . .'** More information on the Amos Bursary can be found here: https://www. amosbursary.org.uk/about/

p.11   **'A recent report by the *Financial Times* . . .'** 'Millenials Poorer Than Previous Generations', Sarah O'Connor, *Financial Times*, 23 February 2018. https://www.ft.com/ content/81343d9e-187b-11e8-9e9c-25c814761640 More information on the wages and living standards of young people can be found here: https://blogs.lse.ac.uk/ politicsandpolicy/real-wages-and-living-standards-the-latest-uk-evidence/

p.12   **'In England, young people are more likely than any other age group to live in unsatisfactory housing . . .'** 'Is

Britain Fairer? The State of Equality and Human Rights 2018', Equality and Human Rights Commission. https://www.equalityhumanrights.com/sites/default/files/is-britain-fairer-accessible.pdf

p.12 'The Office for National Statistics . . .' https://www.ons.gov.uk/peoplepopulationandcommunity/crimeandjustice/articles/thenatureofviolentcrimeinenglandandwales/yearendingmarch2018

Identity

p.20 'I think this is also true . . .' https://yougov.co.uk/topics/politics/articles-reports/2018/06/18/young-people-are-less-proud-being-english-their-el The same poll does however suggest that when it comes to 'Britishness' as opposed to 'Englishness', there is no significant variation between young and old people.

p.21 'Britain is my home, my nationality, my frame of reference . . .' 'This Country of Mine Always Made Me Feel Like I Didn't Belong', Afua Hirsch, *Financial Times*, 26 January 2018. https://www.ft.com/content/84b4c0a2-0097-11e8-9650-9c0ad2d7c5b5

p.23 'Most people are familiar with the Afrobeat styles . . .' 'The Rise of Afrobeats', Dan Hancox, *Guardian*, 19 January 2012. https://www.theguardian.com/music/2012/jan/19/the-rise-of-afrobeats

p.38 'This isn't just the case with Syrian refugees . . .' International Migration Report, United Nations. https://www.un.org/en/development/desa/population/migration/publications/migrationreport/docs/MigrationReport2017_Highlights.pdf

p.38 'Perhaps most surprisingly . . .' https://www.un.org/en/development/desa/population/publications/pdf/popfacts/PopFacts_2017-5.pdf

p.43 'The Windrush scandal came to light . . .' 'Windrush
Scandal: No Passport for Thousands Who Moved to
Britain', Amelia Gentleman, *Guardian*, 4 May 2018.
https://www.theguardian.com/uk-news/2018/may/04/
windrush-scandal-no-passport-for-thousands-who-
moved-to-britain

p.44 'According to the Office of National Statistics . . .' https://
www.ons.gov.uk/peoplepopulationandcommunity/
populationandmigration/internationalmigration/
datasets/populationoftheunitedkingdombycountry
ofbirthandnationality

Home

p.57 'The Education Policy Institute define disadvantage . . .'
https://epi.org.uk/wp-content/uploads/2018/07/EPI-
Annual-Report-2018-Lit-review.pdf

p.63 'A recent research project conducted by . . .' 'Housing
Crisis Affects Estimated 8.4 million in England -
Research', 23 September 2019. https://www.bbc.co.uk/
news/uk-49787913

p.64 'According to the website for the Office . . .' Office of the
United Nations High Commissioner for Human Rights,
www.ohchr.org

p.65 'Not long ago, I came across an even more shocking
statistic . . .' 'Shipping Containers Being Used to House
Children as "More Than 200,000 Go Without Homes",
Report Says', Jacob Jarvis, *Evening Standard*, 21 August
2019. https://www.standard.co.uk/news/uk/shipping-
containers-being-used-to-house-children-as-more-
than-200000-go-without-homes-report-says-a4217871.html

p.65 'In December 2019, a *Guardian* report . . .' 'Homeless
Households in England Rise by 23% in a Year', Mattha
Busby, *Guardian*, 18 December 2019.

p.74 'In 2018, the Equality Trust . . .', 'The Scale of Economic Inequality in the UK', www.equalitytrust.org.uk/scale-economic-inequality-uk

p.75 'It's hard to overstate . . .' https://www.trustforlondon.org.uk/data/key-facts-london-poverty-and-inequality/df

p.80 'In the 1970s . . .' https://www.ifs.org.uk/uploads/publications/bns/BN178.pdf#page=9

p.80 'A recent report from the right-leaning think tank . . .' https://www.theguardian.com/society/2019/feb/08/million-more-young-adults-live-parents-uk-housing

p.81 'However, as Shelter points out . . .' https://england.shelter.org.uk/housing_advice/homelessness/rules/what_is_homelessness

p.81 'Shelter have estimated that . . .' 'At Least 320,000 Homeless People in Britain, Says Shelter', Patrick Butler, *Guardian*, 22 November 2018. https://www.theguardian.com/society/2018/nov/22/at-least-320000-homeless-people-in-britain-says-shelter

p.82 'As Polly Neate, the chief executive of Shelter . . .' 'Nearly a Million More Young Adults Now Live With Parents', Aamna Mohdin, *Guardian*, 8 February 2019. https://www.theguardian.com/society/2019/feb/08/million-more-young-adults-live-parents-uk-housing

Education

p.87 'One afternoon when I was doing a bit of research for this chapter . . .' 'Working-Class Children Get Less of Everything in Education - Including Respect', Donna Ferguson, *Guardian*, 21 November 2017. https://www.theguardian.com/education/2017/nov/21/english-class-system-shaped-in-schools

p.91 'A 2019 survey by the National Education Union (NEU) of 8,600 school leaders . . .' 'Tired, Hungry and

Shamed: Pupil Poverty "Stops Learning" ', Sally Weale, *Guardian*, 14 April 2019. https://www.theguardian.com/education/2019/apr/14/tired-hungry-shamed-pupil-poverty-stops-learning and https://neu.org.uk/press-releases/state-education-child-poverty

p.93 **'In another recent survey carried out by the NEU . . .'** 'Teachers in England Have "Unmanageable" Job - Global Survey', Richard Adams, *Guardian*, 19 June 2019. https://www.theguardian.com/education/2019/jun/19/teachers-in-england-have-unmanageable-job-global-survey and http://www.oecd.org/education/talis/

p.93 **'A *Guardian* investigation in March 2019 revealed . . .'** ' "It's Dangerous": Full Chaos of Funding Cuts in England's Schools Revealed', Sally Weale and Richard Adams, *Guardian*, 8 March 2019. https://www.theguardian.com/education/2019/mar/08/its-dangerous-full-chaos-of-funding-cuts-in-englands-schools-revealed

p.95 **'In a 2018 National Education Union survey, nine in ten teachers agreed . . .'** https://neu.org.uk/press-releases/sats-do-not-benefit-childrens-learning-and-are-bad-their-well-being-neu-survey

p.95 **'Irrespective of how well they fare in tests, 49 per cent . . .'** https://www.cbi.org.uk/media-centre/articles/half-of-young-people-do-not feel-prepared-for-world-of-work-cbi-accenture-hays-survey/

p.106 **'Is it any wonder . . .'** https://www.ymca.org.uk/latest-news/cuts-to-youth-services-to-reach-breaking-point-during-critical-time-for-youth-community-support

p.121 **'A recent** BBC **report concluded that . . .'** https://www.bbc.co.uk/news/education-46541454

p.121 **'One consequence of this is that between 2010 and 2018 there was a 35 per cent decrease in arts entries at GCSE . . .'** https://www.sec-ed.co.uk/news/tate-warning-over-decline-in-arts-education/ and https://www.

theguardian.com/commentisfree/2019/mar/12/the-guardian-view-on-humanities-degrees-art-for-societys-sake and https://culturallearningalliance.org.uk/further-decline-in-arts-gcse-and-a-level-entries/

p.122 'The government's own data shows . . .' https://www.ethnicity-facts-figures.service.gov.uk/education-skills-and-training/absence-and-exclusions/pupil-exclusions/latest#permanent-exclusions-by-ethnicity

p.123 'In the short-term . . .' https://www.ippr.org/files/2017-10/making-the-difference-summary-october-2017.pdf

p.123 'This is one of many reasons that . . .' 'Saving Troubled Teenagers is a Tale of Two Cities', David Cohen, *Evening Standard*, 6 January 2020. https://www.standard.co.uk/news/education/saving-troubled-teenagers-is-a-tale-of-two-cities-a4327386.html

p.123 'Beyond the cost to the individuals involved . . .' https://www.ippr.org/files/2017-10/making-the-difference-summary-october-2017.pdf

p.123 'However, all data shows that schools are generally moving . . .' https://www.thersa.org/discover/publications-and-articles/rsa-blogs/2019/08/exclusions

Justice

p.137 'According to official figures from the Office for National Statistics . . .', 'London Knife Crime Hits Record High', Martin Bentham, *Evening Standard*, 23 January 2020. https://www.standard.co.uk/news/crime/knife-crime-england-london-hits-record-high-a4342451.html

p.139 'And if that is racial prejudice, then I am guilty . . .' A link to an *Independent* report on Boris Johnson's original *Guardian* column here: https://www.independent.co.uk/news/uk/politics/boris-johnson-bunch-black-kids-racist-column-guardian-a9213356.html p.139 **'I am a young black man, which means . . .'** https://www.ethnicity-facts-figures.service.gov.uk/crime-justice-and-the-law/policing/stop-and-search/latest

p.139 **'Stop and search is consistently ineffective at reducing violent crime . . .'** 'Met Police "Disproportionately" Use Stop and Search Powers on Black People', Vikram Dodd, *Guardian*, 26 January 2019. https://www.theguardian.com/law/2019/jan/26/met-police-disproportionately-use-stop-and-search-powers-on-black-people

p.150 **'Of the 29,000 complaints lodged within one year, only 100 were managed by the Commission . . .'** https://www.theguardian.com/society/2009/apr/08/police-complaints-commission

p.150 **'In 2017 alone, twenty-three people died in police custody . . .'** 'Police Custody in England and Wales', Vikram Dodd, *Guardian*, 25 July 2018. https://www.theguardian.com/uk-news/2018/jul/25/highest-number-of-people-in-a-decade-die-in-police-custodyPublished in July 2018.

p.151 **'In a piece in the *Guardian* . . .'** ' "The Worst of All Outcomes" ', John Crawley, *Guardian*, 8 April 2009. https://www.theguardian.com/society/2009/apr/08/police-complaints-commission

p.153 **'The new IOPC can discipline officers directly . . .'** 'New Police Watchdog Launches Inquiry', Lizzie Dearden, *Independent*, 8 January 2018. https://www.independent.co.uk/news/uk/crime/police-watchdog-launch-iopc-replace-ipcc-independent-office-for-police-conduct-uk-public-a8147696.html

p.153 **' "I do not accept the findings . . ." '** 'Rashan Charles' Great Uncle, Former Met Officer Rod Charles', Rod Charles, *Hackney Gazette*, 24 July 2018. https://www.hackneygazette.co.uk/news/rashan-charles-uncle-rod-charles-avoidable-deaths-following-police-contact-will-increase-1-5620448 p.153 **'Acting on behalf of Charles' family . . .'** 'Rashan Charles: Family "Extremely Disappointed" by IOPC Findings and are Considering Legal Challenge', Sam Gelder, *Hackney Gazette*, 22 August 2018. https://www.hackneygazette. co.uk/news/crime-court/rashan-charles-family-extremely-disappointed-iopc-considering-challenge-dalston-1-5653645

p.154 **'According to police data, a black person is four times more likely . . .'** https://www.bbc.co.uk/news/ uk-england-london-44214748

p.154 **'The number of assaults on officers on active duty have risen by a third between 2015 and 2019 . . .'** https:// assets.publishing.service.gov.uk/government/uploads/ system/uploads/attachment_data/file/539200/hosb0516-assaults.pdf

p.164 **'A compelling example of this . . .'** From 'In Care, Out of Trouble' http://www.prisonreformtrust.org.uk/Portals/0/ Documents/In%20care%20out%20of%20trouble%20 summary.pdf

p.164 **'At the moment, prisons are not safe . . .'** https://assets. publishing.service.gov.uk/government/uploads/system/ uploads/attachment_data/file/797074/safety-custody-bulletin-q4-2018.pdf

p.165 **'According to recent figures . . .'** http://www. prisonreformtrust.org.uk/Portals/0/Documents/ Bromley%20Briefings/Prison%20the%20facts%20 Summer%202019.pdf

p.165 **'In 2019, it cost, on average . . .'** https://assets.publishing. service.gov.uk/government/uploads/system/uploads/ attachment_data/file/841948/costs-per-place-costs-per-prisoner-2018-2019.pdf

p.166 **'One of the statistics that stood out to me . . .'** This Kenny Report and others can be accessed via the

following link: http://www.kennyreport3.com/pdf/
KennyReport1.pdf

p.168 **'Why have murders plummeted in Scotland . . .'** 'Ten
Charts That Show the Rise of Knife Crime in England in
Wales', Danny Shaw, BBC, 18 July 2019. https://www.bbc.
co.uk/news/uk-42749089

p.169 **'A second element of Scotland's approach . . .'** 'Is There a
Link Between Scotland's Exclusion Rate and Knife
Crime', Nichola Rutherford, BBC, 8 March 2019. https://
www.bbc.co.uk/news/uk-scotland-47484927

p.173 **'I remember reading about Operation Trident . . .'**
https://www.ethnicity-facts-figures.service.gov.uk/
uk-population-by-ethnicity/national-and-regional-
populations/population-of-england-and-wales/latest

p.173 **'Government statistics show that . . .'** https://assets.
publishing.service.gov.uk/government/uploads/system/
uploads/attachment_data/file/849200/statistics-on-race-
and-the-cjs-2018.pdf

p.174 **Another recent study by . . .'** 'Racial Bias in Stop and
Search Getting Worse, Report Reveals', Mark Townsend,
Guardian, 13 October 2018. https://www.theguardian.
com/law/2018/oct/13/racial-bias-police-stop-and-search-
policy-black-people-report

Business

p.180 **'The government's own commission . . .'** https://assets.
publishing.service.gov.uk/government/uploads/system/
uploads/attachment_data/file/798687/SMC_State_of_
Nation_2018-19_Summary.pdf

p.189 **'The Wolf of Walthamstow . . .'** 'Teenage Tuck Shop
Entrepreneur', Kenza Bryan, *Independent*, 14 July 2017.
https://www.independent.co.uk/news/uk/home-news/

wolf-walthamstow-entrepeneur-tuck-stop-teenage-youth-charity-profits-nathan-john-baptiste-15-year-a7841546.html

p.189 **'Or there's Bejay Mulenga . . .'** 'Meet Bejay Mulenga', Tommy Williams, Forbes, 19 November 2019. https://www.forbes.com/sites/tommywilliams1/2019/11/19/meet-bejay-mulenga-24-year-old-entrepreneur-helping-fortune-500-companies-engage-with-gen-z/#41e4a4df156c

p.195 **'The headline read . . .'** https://www.independent.co.uk/news/media/tv-radio/radio-1-teen-hero-head-of-youth-council-called-in-to-help-boss-ben-cooper-44-bridge-the-generation-10128834.html

p.207 **'In 2016, the year I created . . .'** https://tradingeconomics.com/united-kingdom/new-businesses-registered-number-wb-data.html

p.207 **'In the same year, 328,000 businesses collapsed . . .'** 'It Pays to Be Pessimistic, Shows New Research Into Entrepreneurs', University of Bath, 3 October 2018. https://phys.org/news/2018-10-pessimistic-entrepreneurs.html

p.216 **'In 2018, there were 381,000 new businesses registered . . .'** https://researchbriefings.files.parliament.uk/documents/SN06152/SN06152.pdf

Politics

p.241 **'As John Sparkes, the CEO . . .'** https://www.crisis.org.uk/about-us/media-centre/politicians-police-and-charities-urge-government-to-scrap-draconian-vagrancy-act/

p.241 **'The government's own statistics . . .'** https://www.crisis.org.uk/about-us/media-centre/number-of-rough-sleepers-in-england-soars-by-165-since-2010/

p.241 'The homeless charity St Mungo's . . .' https://www.
connection-at-stmartins.org.uk/facts-about-
homelessness/why-is-homelessness-increasing/

p.242 'That's right. In August 2019 . . .' 'Chicken Boxes to Return
to Home Office With Handwritte Knife Crime Solutions',
Guardian, 19 August 2019. https://www.theguardian.com/uk-
news/2019/aug/19/chicken-boxes-home-office-knife-crime

p.244 'However, when pollsters like Opinium . . .' https://www.
opinium.co.uk/
did-young-people-bother-to-vote-in-the-eu-referendum/

p.249 'I grew up in a decade that saw funding . . .' 'Youth
Services Suffer 70% Funding Cut in Less Than a Decade',
Sally Weale, *Guardian*, 20 January 2020. https://www.
theguardian.com/society/2020/jan/20/youth-services-suffer-
70-funding-cut-in-less-than-a-decade

p.250 'One of these is an amazing organisation . . .' More
information on Bite the Ballot here: https://www.
bitetheballot.co.uk/

Charity

p.261 'In 2017 alone, 20.1 million people in the . . .' https://assets.
publishing.service.gov.uk/government/uploads/system/
uploads/attachment_data/file/738261/Community_Life_
Survey_2017-18_Formal_Volunteering_fact_sheet.pdf

Additional Resources

If you would like further information on any of the issues discussed in *Dreaming in a Nightmare*, or would like to help support any of the initiatives and projects discussed, please visit the book's page at:

www.penguin.co.uk

Acknowledgements

I am beyond thankful to everyone who made this book a possibility!

First of all, I want to thank God. Thank you to Tom Avery, my book editor. He brought out the best in me and helped me discover my writing abilities. Thank you to Theophina Gabriel for your assistance.

I want to thank all of our amazing contributors:

Precious Oyelade
Debbie Antwi
Karl Lokko
Victor Acquah
Krystal Frimpong

Seven Jacobs

Mariam Diaby

Damani Mensah

Deborah Emmanuel

Esther Daniel

Daryl Parker

I want to say a big thanks to my immediate family. Mum, Elijah, Deborah, and Josiah. Thank you for supporting me in all that I do. Without your patience and support I wouldn't be where I am today.

To my Imhotep family. Moses, Xavier, Richie, Mayz, you helped me follow my dream.

To the Soho Agency, thank you for helping make this happen. Shout out to the best book agent in the world Ben Clark.

I wanted to say a huge thank you to Vanessa Branson, who helped me get off to a great start with the book. We had a writing camp in which we focused on my introduction. This definitely got me off to a great start.

A big thank you to my family and EMNL Group team. Seven, Kome Asiababor and Johannah Fadiro thank you for your amazing contributions! Nicola Coaker, Robbie Bin-Luboya, William Callaghan, Gesica Popa, Marnie Edwards, Dani Carroll, Munnaser, Krystal Mamongo – thank you all for your help.

Thank you to Ajaz & Sam at AKQA, who gave me a shot as a young entrepreneur.

To the Big Change and Virgin teams thanks for the continued support. Essie North, Noah Devereux, Noah Bernstein, Freddie Morton-Hooper, Caitlin Ross, Sarina Hancock. Shout out to Ayo, Kobby, and Rhubi.

Thank you to all of my friends who have also supported. From Christ Church Primary School, Archbishop Tenison's School, and St Francis Xavier College. Thank you to my teachers for their belief and encouragement throughout my years, Mr Wong, Mr Reid, Miss Walker, Miss Donna, Mr Bromfield, Miss Gordon, Mrs Sims, Mr Fynn, Miss Sally and Ms Arnold, Mr Thomas, Mr Williams.

Thank you to Simon Ettingshausen, Keisha Bambury, Dionne Constantinious, 7Coy, South-East London ACF. Shout out to all of my fellow cadets at 71.

To Diane, thank you for bringing out my passion for politics. Thank you for providing me with early opportunities.

Richie Montana you are the G.O.A.T., thanks for giving the greatest life advice.

To Desi and Vanessa, thank you for your commitment to change lives. Thank you for what you've done for Adewunmi. Thank you to Fashion for Relief.

To the Okogwu family, Aunty, Uncle, Marian, Eve and Chi Chi. Thank you for your support. Marian thank you for your early guidance and supporting me in my growth and progression.

Big thank you to Lord Hastings, Kenny Imafidon, and the whole Men of Purpose group.

Uncle Mark, Joel, Paul and the entire team at The Conduit.

Jussy, Theo, Thea, we did it. Teamwork makes the dreamwork.

Nelson Abbey, thank you for your advice and support.

Monty, Adrian, Rens, Nicola, the Nike and Converse teams, thank you for supporting me through my business

Thank you to Christ is the Ladder Ministries and Divine Sanctuary, my place of hope. Pastor Toyin Aderele and Pastor Nike, Pastor Olamosun. I want you to know my appreciation

I would like to give a big thanks to my Aunts Leti, Harriet, Florence, Sanatu and Sandra. Thanks also to my Godfather Faith Child.

A big thanks to Disturbing London records and their entire team. Dumi Oburota thank you!

Relentless Records, Ben Coates, thank you for believing in me, and giving me a shot. Thank you to Shabs, Ewan, Rob, Tia, and the rest of the team for all of your help.

Big thank you to Abbi Oakley. I am grateful for your support.

Lyande Kaikai thank you for your business mentoring and support. Thank you for your guidance and continuous support Faith Child.

Thanks for being a mentor to me Fikky. Big thank you to Samuel Ade for your wisdom.

A want to say a huge thank you to the whole team at Penguin. Thank you for putting up with me in your office space and for helping me bring this book to life:

Kate McQuaid
Emma Wallace
Natalia Cacciatore
Lemara Lindsay-Prince
Joanna Taylor
Michael Walker
Steph Heathcote
Eoin Dunne
Tallulah Lyons
Anna Cowling
Sophie Whitehead
Etty Eastwood

And finally, the one and only Jeanette Slinger. You are amazing and I love you to bits!

There are six people that I need to spend a bit of time thanking. People who have done more for me than I can ever repay them for:

Remy Blumenfeld

Remy, without you, the book would not be possible. Thanks for giving me the space and time to work on the manuscript, and for all your support and guidance.

Tinie Tempah

Thank you for seeing something in me, when I was only thirteen! You have changed my life, and given me the ability to dream. For that I am forever grateful.

Maduka Okeke

Thank you for not driving off when I jumped in front of your car! Your early support and continued investment in me and my projects have got me to where I am.

Nachson Mimran

Nachson, you are a rock star! I knew you were special from the first time I met you. Your work and your ideas have made me believe that real change in the world is possible.

Holly Branson

You gave me my first chance when I turned up to interview you with only my broken BlackBerry! Since that day you've given me more opportunities than I can remember, and many more than I can properly thank you for. I'm eternally grateful.

Kelly Okogwu

Kelly, all of this is really down to you. This book is your idea, and it would not be here without your amazing guidance and help. You've always made me feel invincible, and always made me feel like nothing is impossible. Thank you.

My last thank you goes to #Merky and Stormzy. Tobe, thank you for giving me a chance to change my future. AK thank you for helping me bring my ideas to life. Stormzy, thank you for using your platform to give a voice to the voiceless and a space for young people who often miss out.

There are many more people to thank than there is room for here. A longer list can be found at www.dreaminginanightmare.com